American
Commencement

Graduation Speeches that Inspired a New Nation

American
Commencement

Michael Farris

PUBLISHING GROUP
www.BHPublishingGroup.com

ISBN: 978-0-8054-3071-4

Published by B&H Publishing Group
Nashville, Tennessee

Dewey Decimal Classification: 815
Subject Heading: CHRISTIAN LIFE \ AMERICAN
SPEECHES \ UNITED STATES—BIOGRAPHY

Scripture verses taken from
the King James Version of the Bible.

1 2 3 4 5 6 7 8 • 15 14 13 12 11

Dedication

To Jim and Cececia, who have enabled so many young
people to be educated for Christ and for liberty.

Acknowledgments

I want to thank Cate Pilgrim Smith for her invaluable research assistance during her senior year at Patrick Henry College

Contents

Preface

Congratulations on your graduation!

Most graduates have a mixture of emotions at this time. You probably have a tremendous sense of relief and accomplishment for finishing a major course of study. You may have a sense of anticipated loss of relationships that will undoubtedly change as friends move and circumstances change.

But almost all graduates experience both a sense of excitement and perhaps a little nervousness about "what comes next."

I have collected a series of graduation speeches from the early days of America to help give you some insight into this very question: What comes next?

When America was young, there was a tremendous national sense of anticipation about the future. It was an era characterized by both great dreams and much uncertainty.

These speeches possess timeless qualities. And America

needs future leaders whose character and convictions parallel those of these early American graduates.

These historic speakers urged the graduates to pursue paths that were designed to lead to personal and national success—even greatness.

There was an apparent tradition to employ the most sophisticated language of the day in these commencement addresses. Much of the meaning of the excellent messages would be lost on us today if the reader had to wade through complex sentences with a dictionary in hand. Accordingly, in response to the excellent suggestion of my editor, I have updated the language of the speeches using a "dynamic" form of "translation"; that is, I have tried to give a concept-by-concept revision rather than merely a word-for-word restatement. The necessity of doing this really does highlight how advanced the founding generation was in its academic prowess.

I cannot pass by this moment without giving you my own best advice for success—and, yes, perhaps the opportunity to do great things. In fact, this is a story I have often told when I have been asked to speak at graduations. It is the best advice I know how to give to a young person who wants to live a life of true significance.

During my junior and senior years of college, I had a wonderful professor of political science, Dr. Dick S. Payne, who taught a number of courses in constitutional law. I loved his classes, took them all, and did well. Sadly, this professor died in my last term of my senior year. Since I was his star student and no one on the faculty felt qualified to teach his courses, the chairman of the department asked me to do the lectures from my notes from Dr. Payne while the chairman sat in the classroom with me. This lasted for a short period until a proper new professor could be found.

This background gave me a lot of confidence going into law school. I was quick to speak up in my classes and was unashamed in arguing for a conservative and traditional interpretation of the Constitution as I had been taught by Dr. Payne.

One Sunday I felt convicted by the Holy Spirit about my behavior in law school. This is the message that rested in my heart: *So everybody in this law school knows you are a constitutional conservative. When are you going to tell anyone that you are a Christian?*

The conviction was as sharp as a knife in my gut.

The next day I took a yellow piece of paper from my legal pad and wrote on it: *Anyone interested in starting a Bible study for law students call Mike Farris* and gave my phone number. That was it. I didn't stand on a street corner and preach. I just posted a sign for a Bible study.

The word quickly circulated that this "Farris guy" was some kind of born-again Christian.

Sometime later I called a local attorney named Ray Eberle to ask him to come to speak at our Bible study. I had heard that Mr. Eberle was a Christian and thought he would be an encouragement to the law students. He quickly accepted saying, "I have heard about your Bible study. Sure, I will speak. Would you like a job?" I said yes.

That was it. That was my entire job interview word for word.

One day when I was parking my car for my job with Wolff & Eberle, one of my classmates saw me from across the street. He was walking in front of the Spokane Opera House in the city's beautiful Riverfront Park. He yelled at me, "Hey, Farris, they have a liquor license application here on the Opera House. We can come here and get drunk together. Ha ha ha ha."

He meant it as good-natured teasing, but he knew that I wasn't into that kind of thing because of my faith.

I went over to read the application, and as I looked into it, I found that there were plans not only for a liquor outlet in the opera house but also in the center of Riverfront Park right next to the children's carnival rides and play area. I looked around the street and could see numerous outlets for liquor sales, and it just seemed to me that the city of Spokane didn't need to get in the business of selling liquor in Riverfront Park.

So I started Citizens Opposed to Opera House Liquor, which I abbreviated as COOL. The press never asked me how many people were members of the group. Actually there were two of us. A woman in her eighties who had been a member of the Women's Christian Temperance Union and me. And we were citizens—and, yes, we were opposed to opera house liquor.

We succeeded in totally blocking the liquor outlet in the children's play area, and selling alcoholic beverages at the opera house was limited to special events.

Because of this activity, some people involved in a statewide pro-family conservative organization asked me to join with them in some other issues—including battles against pornography. I worked on those issues and was sent to a conference in New York City to learn how to battle the porn industry.

Because of these activities I developed a number of friends who were involved in an ever wider number of political and legal issues.

One morning in 1978, one of these friends called me to tell me that Congress had just voted to change the rules for the ratification of the Equal Rights Amendment. Thirty-five states had ratified the amendment, which was three short of the number needed to add the amendment to the Constitution. So the feminists had convinced Congress to change the language in the proposed amendment to eliminate the seven-year deadline (that was about to expire) and to give more than three additional years to obtain the ratification.

My friend asked, "Mike, do you think this is constitutional?"

"No," I replied. "Clearly not."

"Well, then, what are you going to do about it?" she asked.

A few days later I was commissioned to bring a constitutional challenge to this act of Congress which had extended the time for ratifying the ERA. My clients were four Washington state legislators.

Sometime later I called Beverly LaHaye to ask her to do a fund-raising event for this lawsuit. She did.

In the meantime I had started the Moral Majority of Washington and organized a big rally where Tim LaHaye was the main speaker.

Shortly after these two events, the LaHayes called me and offered me a full-time job as the general legal counsel for Beverly's new group, Concerned Women for America.

I was working with the LaHayes when they interviewed Dr. Raymond Moore about homeschooling. Dr. Moore cornered me and talked me into homeschooling my own children.

As a result of this, I started Home School Legal Defense Association. I have had a part in helping to change the law on homeschooling all over the nation. I was named one of the top one hundred "Faces of Education" for the entire twentieth century because of my work in homeschooling.

Because of these activities, I was able to run for statewide political office, argue in the Supreme Court of the United States, argue in dozens of appellate courts all over the country, help fight for religious freedom in Communist countries, help legalize homeschooling in other nations, serve as the founding president of Patrick Henry College, and became friends with numerous leaders (including President George W. Bush who calls me "Mikey.")

I have been privileged to be involved in a lot of things the world counts as significant.

Here is the key. I can draw a straight line from all of these exciting activities—and yes, many successes—all the way back to that yellow piece of paper announcing a Bible study for law students.

Everything, and I mean everything, that I have been privileged to do in my career came as a direct result of being willing to stand up for Christ on that one occasion in law school.

God said to one of His servants, "You have been faithful with a few things; I will put you in charge of many things" (Matt. 25:21 NIV).

To be sure, I have faced many additional times where I had a choice of whether I was going to remain faithful to Christ. And while I am far from perfect, I have consistently chosen publicly to identify with God and His people.

God has rewarded my meager faithfulness with the opportunity to participate in significant activities that are all out of proportion to any merit in me. His rewards and the opportunities I have had are far greater than I could ever have imagined.

God earnestly wants people to do great things. Here is

the secret to be an instrument He can use: Be faithful in little things.

Michael Farris

Heroes Who Inspire
Samuel Davies

1

Introduction

We have many good reasons to consider men like Patrick Henry and George Washington as great American heroes. We are inspired by their stories and guided by their ideas. Who were their heroes? Who did their teachers hold before them as heroes with the kind of character and ideals they should pursue? Samuel Davies, who was Patrick Henry's boyhood pastor, uses one of the great heroes of the faith, King David, to inspire the leaders of early America.

Background

Thirty-six-year-old Samuel Davies had a reputation throughout the colonies as a preacher of iron will and impeccable character. Although he could not afford to go to college, Delaware-born Davies spent his teens preparing for the ministry at a Presbyterian church in Pennsylvania under the supervision of Samuel Blair. By age twenty-three, Davies was visibly making good on his resolve "that while life and sufficient strength remained, he would devote himself earnestly to the work of preaching the gospel." Not only had his hometown presbytery in New Castle County granted him a license to preach, but the church board had also ordained him as an evangelist to Virginia. At age thirty-six he became president of Princeton, although he is best remembered as a Presbyterian minister.

Freshly ordained, Davies threw himself into ministry with remarkable fervor, writing and preaching sermons with such intensity that he jeopardized his health. He would ride hours on horseback, braving the rugged terrain of Virginia and Pennsylvania to visit his scattered congregations. Despite an ongoing battle against tuberculosis, Davies managed to pastor seven churches spread throughout five counties.

However, Davies yearned for greater unity not just among his local churches but across the entire Presbyterian denominational movement in the colonies. He founded and was appointed the first moderator of the Presbytery of Hanover, a forum of Presbyterian ministers from every congregation in Virginia and North Carolina. Davies was the leader they were looking for, a passionate Christian with a firebrand approach to the gospel. When George Whitefield inspired the New Light Presbyterian movement, Davies fully supported him and began following Whitefield's method of presenting the gospel as a choice where "you must be born again."

Davies labored tirelessly from the pulpit, from which vantage point young Patrick Henry first heard him. Davies's passionate oratory impressed the future statesman, and Henry remembered standing in the back of his father's wagon on the ride home from church trying to repeat Davies's sermons word for word. Themes of liberty, freedom, and duty must have resonated with Henry's own patriotic soul; and Henry himself credits Davies with influencing his speaking style. Doubtlessly, after he outgrew the wagon, Patrick Henry would have owned a collection of Davies's sermons, which went through four editions in the United States and nine editions in England and was a popular volume for decades after Davies's death. Throughout the years preceding the American Revolution, Davies was considered "the animating soul" in the fight for religious liberty in the colonies of Virginia and North Carolina.

In 1753 Davies and another Presbyterian minister voyaged to Great Britain and Ireland on a fund-raising mission for the college at Princeton. Despite a miserable voyage from Philadelphia to London (complete with toothache and seasickness), Davies and his fellow preacher collected sufficient funds for the construction of Nassau Hall and other campus buildings.

A few years after his return from that trip to his home church in Virginia, Samuel Davies was nominated to succeed Jonathan Edwards as president of Princeton (which until 1896 was known as the College of New Jersey). It was no surprise that he accepted the presidency in 1759, but his death from pneumonia a short eighteen months later came as a shocking blow to the college and the larger Presbyterian community. Davies, only thirty-eight at his death, still managed to leave a legacy to the students at Princeton. He had the college library catalogued, raised the standards for admission, made the bachelor's degree more difficult to attain, and required members of the senior class to present lectures and orations to the rest of the student body. However, in addition to his strict academic policies, Davies left behind several melodious odes to peace and science which became commencement sing-alongs.

Davies's advice to the eleven members of the class of 1760 still rings true today: "Whatever be your place," he told the young men he had taught as seniors, "imbibe and cherish a public spirit. Serve your generation." His words certainly did not fall on deaf ears; among those eleven was a member of the Continental Congress, the founder of a college in North Carolina, a member of the United States House of Representatives, and Benjamin Rush, who signed the Declaration of Independence.

Speech

Samuel Davies
Nassau-Hall, Princeton
September 21, 1760

A Valedictory Address to the Senior Class

David, after he had served his own generation by the will of God, fell on sleep, and was laid unto his fathers, and saw corruption.

—Acts 13:36

Great and good character is often formed by imitation. And if we would shine in any sphere of life, we must consider some examples of illustrious men who have preceded us. Great generals have acquired their military skill by careful study of the memoirs of Alexander the Great and Caesar of former ages. And if we would rise to the heights of greatness in writing, we must always remember Homer, Plato, Demosthenes, or Cicero. And, though we may not achieve such fame, how shall we form our characters to become an amiable, good, useful, and public-spirited person?

After careful study, I can find no example that appears to me more pertinent or useful, than the example of David:

- A man characterized by the highest accolade to

which human nature can aspire: conformity to God who is the standard of all perfection. David is called a man after God's own heart.

- A man, though he lacked the advantages of a noble birth or formal education and had no training in the flattery or guile of a courtier, rose to the height of human grandeur and became an extensive blessing to the work of both God and country.

In David there was a combination of exalted characteristics that have shone brightly through all ages. Each of his splendid accomplishments radiates like a facet on a rare and beautiful diamond. He was an invincible hero in the field of battle; a magnificent and good king on the throne; a great example of loyalty under persecution; a devout and sublime poet; and to finish all, the servant of God and his generation. He suffered, he fought, he reigned, he prophesied, he sang, he performed everything to serve his generation, according to the will of God.

The excellence of the example of David consists in two things, a *public spirit* and *true religion*. The union of these two qualities ever marks the truly good and useful person. So inseparably are these united that the one cannot exist in the entire absence of the other. They form a beautiful symmetry; they contain the substance of all obedience to the divine law, which is summed up in the love of God and the love of man. And if you, my dear young graduate, lay these qualities of public spirit and true religion as your heart's foundation for future useful and important service, then my highest wishes will be accomplished in you. It will be a blessing to the world that ever you passed through it.

Whatever your station in life, permit me to plant this important instruction as a seed in your heart: embrace and cherish a public spirit. Serve your generation. Live not for yourselves but for the public. Be the servants of the church; the servants of your country, your nation, the whole race of mankind, even your enemies. Let such service be a vigorous and unrelenting effort for your whole life so that you will leave the world wiser and better than you found it at your entrance. Let your own ease, your own pleasure, and your own private interests yield to the common good. For this goal, spare no pains; avoid no labor; fear no suffering. For this do everything; suffer everything. For this live and die. Let no selfish passion mislead you, no ungratefulness from others discourage you; let no opposition deter you, no private interest bribe you. To this yield your bodies, your souls, your estates, your life—all that you hold sacred. Bravely live and die, serving your generation—your own generation—just as David did.

"He served his own generation"—every person's sphere of usefulness is limited. Your contemporaries, particularly your countrymen, who are within the reach of your influence, should be the more direct and immediate objects of your good works. This is your day: now you have room upon the stage of life. A long succession of generations has retired into the "chambers of the grave" to give place to you. It is now your turn to act your part. You are surrounded with "a great cloud of witnesses"; the eyes of heaven and earth are fixed upon you in eager expectation and anxious suspense for the result. Therefore strain every muscle to the utmost level of exertion, and act your part well that you may gain the commendation of God, angels, and good men and women. It is but little time you have to work. The "day of life" is short; and the "shadows of evening" are advancing fast, even toward the youngest of you. A neglected opportunity is lost forever, and past omissions can never be supplied by future diligence. Therefore, work while it is called day.

Therefore, my young friends, let true religion be the source of your good will and public spirit; and always adhere to the will of God in all your good services to your fellow man. Let it not be your principal aim to satisfy your own sense of good will, or to secure honor for yourselves, or to accomplish some goal of significance; but make it your goal to please God. Let your desire to please God be the center, in which all the actions of your life shall be grounded and the definition of the length and breadth of your endeavors. Then you may claim a character more noble than even that of patriot; you will be called by an even higher name: Christian.

Enter the world with a deep sense of your mortality; and that after a few turns upon the stage you must retire into the "chambers of death." This is the end of all flesh; and the highest endowments, natural, acquired or supernatural, which even David was adorned with, can be no security against it. Make it the great "business of life" to prepare for death, and for that end begin to meditate on your own life's end. Look forward to approaching death; look downward into the gaping grave, even in the carefree hours of health and youth. And oh! Above all, frequently assess your place in God's eternal world that lies beyond death and the grave. There you must arrive before long. You are today young immortals! You are candidates for eternity! You are heirs of heaven or else of hell! You must dwell forever with Abraham, Isaac, and Jacob in the kingdom of God or with Judas and other sons of perdition in the infernal prison. Unless you secure a happy immortality in Christ, these few uncertain years of life, together with your reason, your liberal education, your religious advantages, and your all, will be nothing more than an everlasting curse. "Strive to enter in at that straight gate"; and do not disappoint my eager hopes of seeing you at the right hand of the Supreme Judge. We are soon to part and be dispersed through the world. But oh! Let us choose heaven as the sure place of our gathering and the commencement of a union never to be dissolved.

Principles of Greatness

John Witherspoon

Introduction

John Witherspoon's graduation message in 1787, the year of our Constitutional Convention, may be the greatest graduation speech in American history.

A few samples help to understand his theme:

> It belongs to magnanimity to attempt great and difficult things.
>
> It belongs to greatness to struggle against difficulties with steadiness and perseverance.
>
> The object of our desires must be just as well as great.

America is the greatest nation in human history. The key

to this greatness is not found in our technology, wealth, or power. But it is found in the greatness of our principles. There is no better explanation of the principles of greatness than this message of John Witherspoon.

Background

Even at age sixty-eight, when he spoke at Princeton's commencement, college president John Witherspoon had presence. One of his students said he had more presence than any other man he had known except for General Washington. It wasn't just Witherspoon's bushy eyebrows, beaky nose, and noticeably large ears that arrested attention; it was his straightforward manner and aura of discipline. When Witherspoon, as a retired college president, addressed the assembled students with a two-hour speech on the pursuit of greatness and Christian virtue, he had followed his normal routine and memorized it. All those students watched an old man mount the podium with no notes and proceeded to listen in amazement as he delivered it from memory. When he told the young men in his audience to "struggle against difficulties with steadiness and perseverance," he wasn't speaking as a greenhorn guide; he had had his share of struggles, many of which occurred during his days as president of Princeton.

John Witherspoon had emigrated from his native Scotland at the request of Benjamin Franklin and Benjamin Rush (despite his wife's terror of crossing the Atlantic), specifically to serve as Princeton's president. Witherspoon was an accomplished scholar who had received his master of arts from Edinburgh University, followed by a master of divinity degree, and a doctorate of divinity from the University of St. Andrews. Throughout his life Witherspoon was an active minister and authored three well-circulated theological treatises, one of which warns Christians to be wary of letting humanistic reasoning supplant a belief in God's sovereign, absolute truth. Another, titled: "A Serious Enquiry into the Nature and Effects of the Stage" (1757), examines the entertainment industry, ultimately concluding that the theater was an "arouser of immoral passion."

In all areas Witherspoon set an example for his students. When he told them patriotism and duty were linked, he practiced what he preached. He served as a member of the Continental Congress, signed the Declaration of Independence (the only member of the clergy to do so), and was a delegate to New Jersey's 1787 ratification convention for the U.S. Constitution. That was Witherspoon's style: lead by example. He told his students to become masters of the English language, and thus in classes and lectures he spoke clearly and forcefully, although he pronounced his words with a crisp Scottish accent that even twenty-odd years in America had not softened.

President Witherspoon saw no reason that faith should not walk hand in hand with reason or that academic studies should not be equally intimate with patriotism.

In 1789 he presided over the first general assembly of the American Presbyterian Church, and that same year a tally of Presbyterian ministers in the colonies revealed Witherspoon's influence: out of a total of 177 Presbyterian ministers in the colonies, ninety-seven were Princeton graduates, and fifty-two of those were Witherspoon's own students!

Princeton grads were also thickly spread in the political arena, and Witherspoon's students included the future President James Madison, future Vice President Aaron Burr, five representatives to the Constitutional Convention, twelve representatives to the Continental Congress, twenty-eight U.S. senators, forty-nine members of the U.S. House of Representatives, three justices of the Supreme Court, eight U.S. district judges, twenty-six state judges, seventeen members of conventions that drew up state constitutions, nine cabinet officers, and twelve state governors.[1] His students' activities got him accused of running a "seminary of sedition," but Witherspoon refused to be daunted. He updated Princeton's curriculum to include the study of Enlightenment thinkers and was an advocate of "common sense" philosophy that incorporated an understanding of man's sin nature. "Others may, if they please, treat the corruption of our nature as a chimera: for my part," Witherspoon said in a 1776 sermon delivered at Princeton, "I see it everywhere, and I feel it every day."[2]

Witherspoon's commitment to truth and liberty did not just inspire his own students. He was a man who impressed great men. After visiting Princeton in 1774, John Adams said of Witherspoon that he was "as high a Son of Liberty, as any man in America." Proudly descended from Scottish reformer John Knox, Witherspoon was a passionate patriot and Christian.

Following the war, Witherspoon spent the last years of his life making repairs to the Princeton campus, which had been badly damaged by occupying British troops. Although he suffered blindness, Witherspoon remained active in the U.S. academic community until his death in 1794. He died on his farm, Tusculum, just outside of Princeton, and his adopted country mourned the loss of a great preacher, scholar, and patriot.

Witherspoon and Madison

John Witherspoon had been president for only a short time when he signed the diploma of a young man named James Madison. It had only been three years since Witherspoon had crossed the ocean from Scotland with his wife and children (and the three hundred books he had compassionately donated to the sadly lacking college library), but Witherspoon had arrived in time to influence future president Madison's moral and academic education.

President Witherspoon's classroom teaching directly contradicted the humanistic writings of his day, and the Princeton curriculum frowned on the deistic, human-reason-is-supreme attitudes of Ben Franklin and Thomas Jefferson. Madison followed suit in this. Witherspoon emphasized the Almighty Power of God; and Madison, though often portrayed as a rationalist, also believed in the supernatural powers of Providence. In a letter to Thomas Jefferson, Madison affirms the miraculous, writing of the incredible harmony that resulted at the Constitutional Convention in Philadelphia, despite disagreements between the large and small states. Despite "a task more difficult than can be well conceived by those who were not concerned in the execution of it," and "the natural diversity of human opinions on all new and complicated subjects," Madison said, "It is impossible to consider the degree of concord which ultimately prevailed as less than a miracle." (To Thomas Jefferson. NEW YORK, October 24, 1787. Writings of Madison, Volume 1: 1769–1793, p. 343.)

Like Witherspoon, Madison believed America was called to act in history upon biblical principles. In 1812 Madison prayed publically that God would inspire all nations with a love of justice and of concord, and with a reverence for the unerring precept of our holy religion, to do to others as they would require that others should do to them; and, finally, that turning the hearts of our enemies from the violence and injustice which sway their councils against us, He would hasten a restoration of the blessings of peace.

Speech

John Witherspoon
Nassau-Hall, Princeton
September 23, 1787

Christian Magnanimity: An Address to the Senior Class Who Were to Receive the Degree of Bachelor of Arts

That ye would walk worthy of God, who hath called you unto his kingdom and glory.

—1 Thessalonians 2:12

Some branches of true religion are universally approved, such as truth and integrity in speech, honesty in dealing, humanity and compassion to persons in distress. But at other times when worldly virtue and Christian virtue seem to be different things. Let us focus on one aspect of these virtues. It can be described as intellectual prowess or greatness of mind. This quality holds a high place in the esteem of all worldly men. It is a virtue of a dazzling appearance; ready to captivate attention, and seems particularly appealing to young persons when they first enter into life.

At the same time, the gospel seems to stand directly opposed to it. The humility of the creature, the abasement and sorrowful repentance of the sinner, the dependence and self-denial of the believer, and the shame and reproach of the cross itself would seem to join together to require us to renounce any attempt to aspire to such greatness of mind.

Is the development of a great mind no virtue at all? Shall we admit that there is a kind of beauty and excellence in mental achievement while confessing at the same time that such pursuits are not properly pursued by the true believer? No! For Scripture points out our original dignity, and the true glory of our nature. Every true Christian starts with humility and repentance but then is taught to aspire after the noblest character and to entertain the most exalted hopes. I hope to be able to show that real greatness is inseparable from sincere faith.

The habitual pursuit of excellence is necessary in order to attempt great and difficult things. Those who from love of slothfulness and a life of ease regularly neglect the exercise or improvement of their mental powers, as well as those who apply their mental capacities with zeal and focus only toward subjects that are vulgar or of small consequence, are plainly lacking in this quality. When any person, endowed with the powers of logic and rational thinking loses them through neglect or destroys them by indulging in sensuality, we say they are acting below themselves. The pursuit of excellence requires the vigorous exertion of all our powers; moreover, it especially requires that we apply ourselves to things of significance and difficulty.

It belongs to greatness to struggle against difficulties with steadiness and perseverance. Perseverance is nothing else but continued and inflexible courage. We see some persons who show the greatest activity and boldness for a season, but time and opposition weakens their force and seems to exhaust their courage as if they wasted the power by the effort. Perseverance, therefore, is necessary to greatness.

Excellence of mind and spirit requires us to encounter dangers with firm resolution. This is inseparable from character. Courage is always considered as a great quality; it has been admired by all mankind in every age. Many, when they speak of a person of greatness, mean nothing else but courage and, when they speak of a person lacking character, have little other idea but that of cowardice. Neither is there any human weakness that is more the object of contempt and disdain than cowardly fear.

It belongs to greatness to bear suffering with fortitude and patience. Such is the state of human life that suffering is, one way or another, unavoidable. Often, difficulties cannot be removed, or enemies cannot be conquered; and then it is the last effort of the greatness of mind to bear up under the weight of the one or the cruelty of the other. A heathen philosopher said a great man, suffering with invincible patience, under a weight of misfortunes, is a sight which even the gods must behold with admiration.

But what is necessary to give excellence of mind real value as a moral and godly virtue? In order to reveal the answer in as clear a light as possible, we will examine the qualities that are necessary for the pursuit of a great mind to be consistent with godly character.

To achieve this quality we must not only seek that which is great; we must also pursue that which is just. Our desires ought to be governed by wisdom and prudence as well as justice. Our actions must be honorable if we want our achievements to be truly illustrious. We have the witness of Christianity as well as our reason and whisperings of our human hearts to tell us that true greatness requires us to pursue only honorable aims and employ only just means. Some of the most powerful human minds have been employed to invade the rights of others instead of promoting the well-being and happiness of others. As the history of the world is little else than the history of human guilt, so many of the most famous names have been those of the most active and successful destroyers of their fellow creatures. Such persons may have had many or most ingredients of natural greatness of mind, but these only served to make their characters more hideous. Moral principles must enter into the composition of true greatness or greatness degenerates into pride, ambition, audacity, ferocity, and obstinacy.

Though it costs him riches or fame, the person who is ready sacrificially to do their duty is one of the most glorious characters we can conceive. At the end of the day, it is not the head or the hands of a person but the heart that is the seat of genuine greatness. Fame and grandeur may not be possible for everyone, but true greatness of mind and soul, which is the fruit of true religion, is a virtue of the heart. Such greatness may be attained by persons from every station of human life, even the most humble.

Sowing and Reaping

Chauncey Whittlesey

3

Introduction

The habits acquired in youth will be the foundation for our lives. When we consistently do what is right, we reap a great reward. When we pursue personal pleasure and sin, we sow seeds of our own destruction.

Background

For nearly thirty years the Reverend Chauncey Whittlesey preached from the pulpit of his New Haven church, following in the footsteps of his father, the Rev. Samuel Whittlesey of Wallingford. From an early age Whittlesey studied theology and public speaking. He graduated from the then tiny

23

Yale College in 1738, and stayed on as a tutor until he became a minister. Whittlesey was proud to be a man with strong convictions, and he took an inflexible approach to school discipline. One of his pupils, missionary David Brainerd, once remarked that Whittlesey had "no more grace than a chair,"[3] for which comment Brainerd was promptly expelled from Yale without a degree. Although Brainerd was at the top of his class at the time, his comment violated a school rule that prohibited the criticism of faculty. Whittlesey, it seems, fully supported the school's decision to expel young Brainerd. Respect for one's elders was something Whittlesey took seriously.

He also took Scripture seriously, and preached fervently in its defense as the inspired Word of God. Occasionally, as with the speech below, Whittlesey was asked to prepare a special message for an event, which text would be printed and circulated after it was delivered. His election speech from 1778 is still studied today, as well as various others from funerals, ordinations, and other special occasions.

In addition to guest lecturing, Whittlesey was also a prolific letter writer. Among his correspondents was Yale graduate Joshua Chandler, who was a member of the general assembly and justice of the peace. Whittlesey was friends with Chandler before the outbreak of the Revolutionary War and was surprised when Chandler declared his allegiance to King George. Chandler had served as New Haven's civil affairs manager and was a member of the state bar. By siding with Mother England, Chandler made himself unpopular in the community and had to flee with his wife and children to British territory in Long Island. To his credit Whittlesey did not wash his hands of Chandler but continued to correspond with him. Chandler grieved over his exile from Connecticut. In a letter to Whittlesey, he wrote nostalgically of his home, longing with "very strong affection" for the land of his birth. Tragically Chandler would not live to see again the green shores of the Confederation of States. In 1783, while on a ship headed for Nova Scotia, Chandler and his entire family died. First, his wife died aboard the ship. Next his young son fell overboard and drowned. Shortly afterward the captain lost control of the vessel amid the rocks at Musquash Point. Chandler was killed by the collision with the rocks, and although his daughter swam safely to shore, she too soon perished from exposure to the winter elements.

This tragedy had a profound impact on Whittlesey, and for a short time the devout minister questioned his faith in the kindness of God. However, just as he was always challenging his pupils and congregation, Whittlesey turned to the promises found in the Bible and did not renounce his faith.

Speech

Chauncey Whittlesey
Yale College
September 12, 1744

A Poem by J. Hubbard precedes the address:

> *If you would be what this discourse design'd,*
> *Some great example always keep in mind;*
> *The Author then before you always place,*
> *And when you read his precepts, view his face.*
> *In them you're only told how to be great,*
> *In him you plainly see this happy state:*
> *Strain every nerve, on ev'ry feature gaze;*
> *The more you imitate, the more you praise:*
> *If near the bright example you arrive*
> *Your names with his shall mouldring time survive.*

These thoughts were penned with a particular purpose for your instruction and benefit; and whatever may be the opinion of mankind in general (whose candid opinion I crave), I give them confidently to you knowing that you will study them with care and delight.

All people are moral agents and are endowed with sufficient capacity and power to know and to do what is right. The parable contained in Matthew 25 teaches that God, the great Giver of all, distributes powers and abilities differently to different moral agents according to his own sovereign and wise pleasure. What is required of the servants in the parable? That they faithfully improve the talents they are entrusted with and that they make great gains thereby. And at last they are amply rewarded by their Lord.

In like manner what God expects of all people is an honest and faithful improvement. This is the true notion of the religious, the virtuous life. And this is the beginning of wisdom.

If we are faithfully to improve the talents we enjoy, since we are rational beings, then we must act consistently with the dignity of our natures, being made in the image of God. Now this presupposes that we aim at good ends and act upon just principles:

- Principles that are intelligent
- Principles that we have examined, understand, and find to be supported by proper evidence
- Principles of importance and worth, that concern our happiness

When we have believed and meditated upon such principles, they cause us to pursue the great and good ends above mentioned.

Our talents will be increased by faithfully implementing what we have learned from the Word of God. What else can be the meaning of the words of the text of the parable? Surely God will not permit his faithfulness to fail; he will completely answer the description given of him in the Sacred Word as a being of unshakable fidelity. Whatever encouragement he has given any of his creatures to trust in him, he will, without a doubt, in every case act fully up to it.

We can be assured from the evidence of experience and observation that our talents will be increased if we faithfully seek to improve upon what we have been given. Experience will teach us that an action, which at first could not be performed except with much difficulty and labor, will with frequent repetition become easy and delightful. This demonstrates that as we studiously seek to know and practice virtue it will become more easily accomplished and will produce great joy.

This is one of the precepts which Pythagoras is said to have taught his disciples: choose the course of life which is most excellent and then pursue it faithfully. It will be made the most delightful of pathways. An action by being frequently practiced will become as familiar and easy as if we were prompted to act by some natural inclination. Yet as our knowledge is increased, so our obligation to practice what is right is also increased.

Those who begin soon, who set out on this business in the morning of their days, in the bloom of life, and apply themselves to the task with vigor and unceasing labor, will flourish like the palm tree and grow like the cedar in Lebanon. You will keep away from dangerous habits which will otherwise take possession and quickly get deeply rooted in the soul.

Our minds are like a garden. Our minds, unless they are tended with prudence and diligence, will quickly become accustomed to do evil. If we neglect this duty to study and labor with hearty consistency, we will become more and more averse to doing what is right. Errors, when they are entertained as truth without a thorough examination, become deeply rooted and have such a sovereign command in the soul that it is almost impossible to get freed from them or to escape their destructive influence. To free oneself of such long-harbored error seems like cutting off a right hand and plucking out a right eye. Removal will not be accomplished but by great pains and sorrow, by repeated severe resolutions, and with the utmost difficulty. It is a point of great wisdom for you to avoid this unhappy condition by being early and earnest in improving the talents with which God has entrusted you.

Consecrated to God

William Smith

4

Introduction

Sadly it is a common notion that the years of one's youth are the time to "sow some wild oats" before settling down. Usually such thoughts lead to a path of sin, sometimes to outright debauchery.

In 1757, William Smith, the president of the College and Academy of Philadelphia (that would be later known as the University of Pennsylvania), urged his students to "consecrate to God the first and best of your days!"

He also argued that by living a life pleasing to God, students would find themselves prepared, if the need should arise, to have the character that was needed to lead the defense of the nation if its liberty was threatened.

Less than twenty years later, America's liberty was indeed challenged by the British crown and its invading army.

The character of its defenders was molded in speeches like this one in 1757.

Background

The University of Pennsylvania was not founded by Benjamin Franklin, although he was instrumental in its success, but rather it was founded by the great evangelist George Whitefield. Franklin himself, widely known for his nontraditional religious beliefs, said of Whitefield, "I knew him intimately upwards of thirty years. His integrity, disinterestedness, and indefatigable zeal in prosecuting every good work I have never seen equaled and shall never see excelled." If you walk onto the campus of that Ivy League university today, you can still read, engraved at the base of Whitefield's statue, the following words of tribute:

> The University of Pennsylvania held its first sessions in a building erected for his congregation, and was aided by his collections, guided by his counsel, inspired by his life.
>
> Zealous advocate and patron of higher education in the American Colonies. The Charity School of 1740, the beginning of the

University of Pennsylvania, was a fruit of his ministry.

It is a testimony to the cooperative spirit of early American education that Ben Franklin was able to work closely with George Whitefield to build up the foundation of this nation's educational institutions. Liberal, deistic Franklin found himself actively recruiting orthodox Christians to staff the new college, and one of Franklin's discoveries was William Smith, a distinguished Scotsman who would go on to become the provost of the college.

William Smith was an Anglican priest who also happened to be rabidly procolonial liberty. He actually served jail time for his criticism of the pacifism of Pennsylvania's Quaker-run colony, but his passion for education drew the attention of Ben Franklin. Franklin chanced upon a 1753 pamphlet on the benefits of education and decided to ask the author to teach at Whitefield's new college. Smith was exactly the kind of man Franklin wanted shaping the young minds in the Colonies; in addition to his honorary doctor of divinity degrees from the University of Oxford and Aberdeen, Smith held degrees from the University College Dublin and was a member of the American Philosophical Society. In 1755 Smith became the first provost of the school, a position he held until 1779.

Speech

William Smith
College and Academy of Philadelphia
May 17, 1757

A Charge Delivered at the College and Academy of Philadelphia to the Young Gentlemen Who Took Their Degrees on that Occasion

Surely to live is serious! And you are now about to step into life and embark into all of its busy scenes. It is fitting, then, that you should pause—a solemn pause—at its doorway and consider well what is expected of you and how you are prepared to perform it.

On the one hand, you will have all the dangers and indiscretions of youth to wrestle with, as you first set out into the world. Since you are untested and inexperienced in the ways of the world, you will be likely to consider yourselves as set loose from the reins of discipline and to look all about with thoughts of great joy and the most buoyant of hopes. At every glance, scenes of breathtaking and ever-changing beauty will open before you. The world will seem to be filled with such a bounty of pleasures that choosing will perplex you.

But take great care! Not all pathways lead to the gardens of joy! Many will only seduce you from the path of virtue by false appearances of happiness and draw you on, promising a bliss that is never real but leads instead to the fool's paradise. It is a deceitful region, which proves at last to be the valley of the shadow of death, where deadly snakes lie in wait.

On the other hand, you will find the world will only be inclined to make small allowances for the mistakes of youth. Much—very much—will be expected from you. You have enjoyed superior opportunities to gain knowledge, and this gives your friends and country every right to expect everything from you that is excellent or praiseworthy.

Oh! Let no part of your future conduct disgrace the education you have received or disappoint the hopes you have so justly raised! Strive to shine forth in every manner of moral excellence. Live consistently with the character and dignity of a soul created to live in the eternal presence of God. The Christian world stands much in need of people who demonstrate inflexible patterns of integrity and perseverance. The nation you have inherited is in great need of such.

Unless the result of your education is seen conspicuously in your lives, what will be its significance to you, or to us? Will it not be deemed to have been a vain effort of furnishing the head rather than a true discipline of the heart and manners?

Consecrate to your God the first and best of your days! When you enjoy health of body, strength of mind, and vigor of spirit, make the pursuits of your heart a noble sacrifice, worthy of being presented to the great Creator of heaven and earth! When our prime years have been devoted to the ways of pleasure and folly, how can we then come to God with any confidence that our later years will achieve their full potential since our bodies will be shackled with the remnants of vice and iniquity? Though heaven be all merciful, it is peculiarly painful to consider thoughtfully the alternative outcomes of such a life. The years that seem best to pursue pleasure are, in truth, the best to be yielded in diligent devotion to God.

Life is short, and whatever we accomplish in these few years will be of real value only when our actions clearly originate from first principles. Beware of valuing yourselves by your temporary possessions or falling into the error of those who think they show the depth of their wisdom by disregarding that sublime system, sent down from heaven by the Son of God. The extent of human knowledge and science is poor at best; and those who know the most know but just enough to convince them of their own ignorance. Though we honor human reason and believe that human virtue dignifies our nature, yet your education here will teach you to fix your hopes on a far more solid foundation. It will teach you that reason, when unenlightened by God, may be fallacious and consequently that virtue will be devious.

I am now to offer you a few plain directions on how to live with the world. If you truly love God, you must necessarily love all the creatures for his sake. Do not create in yourself a narrow unfeeling heart, coiled up in its own limited orb. Yet if you wish to be useful to the world, beware of mixing too indiscriminately in its ways or becoming too cheap in the assessment of the common man. But when you are in the world, be cordial to all, familiar with few, cautious in contracting friendships, steadfast in preserving them, and entering into none without the purest virtue in both foundations and goals.

Maintain a dignity of conduct, show evenness of temper, preserve a cheerfulness of countenance, never pretending to appear better than you are. The Christian life, far from being gloomy and severe, was meant to exalt our human nature and show it in its best perfection—happy and joyful.

When you mix in public, you will often have occasion to be disgusted with the vanity and course jesting of the general run of conversation. Strive, therefore, as often as you can to turn the discussion to that which is pure and helpful, regarding always the propriety of time and place. And if you are obliged to speak against what you hear, let it be evident to all that you are offended, not at the persons but at the things. Great delicacy is requisite in such cases; and you must blame without anger in order to remove the offense and not to wound the offender.

On occasion you may make bold statements that arise from a strong conviction of an important truth and from an awareness of superior knowledge. You may then be perceived as speaking from anger or arrogance despite your good intentions. But if, from the general tenor of your conduct, you have convinced others of the goodness of your heart, such bursts of passion will be forgiven by your friends or considered only as the fire from the flint; "which being smitten, emits its hasty spark and is straightaway cool again."

You will demonstrate your wisdom, however, if you preserve a serene temper, to avoid little disputes and to raise yourselves above the fray, as much as possible. But some things will demand your most vigilant attention, and on some occasions to be silent or consenting would be criminal cowardice with no pretense of virtue.

Should your country call, or should you see the corruptors or corrupted imposing their will upon the public, undermining the civil and religious principles of our country, and gradually paving the way to certain slavery, by spreading destructive notions of government—then, oh then, be nobly roused! Devote your all—eye and ear, and heart, and voice, and hand—in a glorious cause! Cry aloud, and charge the field of battle without the slightest pause, fearless of danger, regardless of opposition, and paying scant attention to the disapproval of the elites in power or to the schemes of villains. Let the world know that liberty is your unconquerable delight and that you are sworn foes to every specter of bondage, either of body or mind!

On Religious Liberty
Barnabas Binney

5

Starting in the 1960s, the religious liberty issues that grabbed national headlines included controversies over Bible reading and prayer in public schools. While these "separation of church and state" battles continue today, there is a new and far more dangerous development.

There is a growing trend toward the coercion of those who disagree with the values of the government out of sincere religious conviction. Doctors who believe that human life is sacred from conception are being forced to perform abortions at the risk of losing their licenses. As a recent beauty contestant learned, a decision to criticize homosexual marriage comes with an enormous cost. Free speech is under assault.

College students are regularly told that secular liberalism led to the freedom of speech and religion. So why do we see this same philosophy closing the doors to a robust practice of these liberties in the name of tolerance?

Could it be that secularism was not the foundation of liberty? Could it be that Christians were the ones who launched this idea? How could Christians be the source of the arguments for liberty since they were the ones doing the persecuting?

This 1774 speech from the College of Rhode Island helps us understand the source of the arguments for liberty then and where they must come from today, if we are to sustain our liberty.

Introduction

Religious liberty was not the dominant policy in the American colonies even on the doorstep of the American Revolutionary War.

In the 1760s in Virginia, a man named John Waller, known as a gambler, abusive in speech, and a persecutor of Baptists, was led to Christ after serving on a jury in a case where a Baptist pastor was prosecuted. Waller became a Baptist minister of some renown and then faced the same kind of persecution he formerly encouraged.

In early 1771, Waller was leading the singing of a psalm during a service in Caroline County, when an Anglican minister and his clerk interrupted the Baptist service. The minister used his whip to try to disrupt the singing of hymns by striking at Waller's hymnal. Since this was not successful, the Anglican cleric shoved his whip in Waller's mouth. The establishment minister then handed Waller over to the sheriff who was standing by. After administering twenty lashes with the whip, the sheriff let him go free.

Waller responded by preaching an extraordinary sermon.

In October 1774, the president of the Baptist-affiliated College of Rhode Island presented a memorial to the Continental Congress at Carpenter's Hall in Philadelphia. College president James Manning urged members to embrace religious liberty for all.

In November 1774, James Madison reported that he had received a report of Baptists being persecuted in New England.

The commencement speech on religious liberty given by a graduate of the College of Rhode Island, Barnabas Binney, was not an oration on a topic that had long been settled. Persecution was still widely practiced by both Anglicans and Puritans.

Binney eloquently proclaims the case for religious liberty, not as a devotee of the Enlightenment but on the clear evidence of the liberty we find in the gospel of Jesus Christ.

* For the complete story of the birth of American religious liberty, see Michael Farris, *From Tyndale to Madison: How the Death of an English Martyr Led to the American Bill of Rights* (B&H Publishing, 2007).

Background

In September 1774 Barnabas Binney graduated from Rhode Island College, which had recently moved campus locations from Warren, Rhode Island, to College Hill overlooking the city of Providence. The proximity of Providence was a lure to students eager to be exposed to city life, but the rigor of the college's classes made a party lifestyle close to impossible. Barnabas Binney recalled that his years at Rhode Island College were "exceedingly full of work," yet records show that Barnabas excelled. Upon receiving his bachelor of arts, Binney "held the first grade in the class" and was asked to give a valedictory speech. Charles Chauncey Binney, the descendant and biographer of Barnabas's son Horace, wrote that Barnabas's valedictory address showed "great freedom as well as fearlessness of thought and proceeded from a mind that was little disposed to submit to any human authority that had not the sanction of reason."

Reason, to Barnabas, could not be divorced from duty, and duty could not be separated from action. He recognized the colonial need for doctors and, after graduating, studied medicine in Philadelphia under Doctor Benjamin Rush. Sometime in 1777, when the Revolutionary Army was in desperate need of physicians, Barnabas volunteered as a hospital surgeon and stayed with Washington's troops during the bitter Valley Forge winter of 1777–1778. In the *American Quarterly Register* of 1839, Binney's descendants remember him as a man of achievement: "His attainments and his embellishments were much above the general state of improvement. His fine intellectual powers, his various and elegant knowledge, his refined and polished manners would alone have given him elevation; while strength of principle—decision and energy of action—sensibility and tenderness, made a combination of qualities engaging to all, and wholly influential and commanding in the circle of domestic friends."

His son Horace also remembers his father as a remarkable man and "an active patriot and scholar." Indeed, Barnabas was a staunch believer in both American government and higher education and sent his son to Harvard. Horace Binney graduated from Harvard in 1797 and was later elected to Congress. Horace in turn sent his son, Horace Binney Jr., to Yale. Barnabas Binney's son and grandson both received the highest honors in their class.

Speech

Barnabas Binney
College of Rhode Island
September, 1774

Religious Liberty's Importance

Religious liberty is the most important subject to both individuals and society. It is the subject most intertwined with the grandest events of kingdoms, nations, and empires. Therefore, it can never be too well understood, too highly prized, or too often taught.

When religious liberty is practiced, it becomes the happy means of uniting the varied interests and different communities of a nation in peaceful harmony. It has ever been found to be the only method of advancing useful and extensive knowledge. It leads to the refinement of the morals of the people and leads them to cherish every virtuous social passion. Honoring this sacred right is the only method of suppressing the brood of vipers who seek to oppress their fellows on matters pertaining to faith or religion.

Those who violate this sacred right reap the most disastrous consequences. Religious tyranny always leads to civil and political tyranny.

By religious liberty we mean a free, uncontrolled liberty of thinking, worshipping, and acting, in all religious matters as we please, provided thereby we are not hurtful to others or to the state. By this we mean that the state may punish those who pursue immorality—such as unlawful disobedience, murder, adultery, theft, perjury, and those overt acts that are injurious to our fellow creatures or society. But punishing a person for the tendency of his principles is wrong because it is punishing people before they are guilty, for fear that they might become guilty.

Those who argue for control of the religious views of others believe and contend that their religious understandings are better and more sensible than others. They may believe that by virtue of their youth, age, piety, superior education, or sheer numbers they are more likely to be in the right than others. To this I reply: Our own personal understanding, be it more or less sensible, is the only faculty which God has given us to separate truth from error. And as every person is accountable to God for our own understanding, not for that of others, our eternal safety consists in not following the direction of others but of our own best judgment before God and his Word.

The first successful strategy of persecutors is to convince the common person that their, the persecutors', interpretation of truth is more likely to be correct than their own.

If someone believes that God and the Scriptures lead to one conviction, but the wise and educated teach another belief, we believe it is always wrong to obey men rather than God.

Christianity, when it was first introduced, contained nothing that was destructive of public peace or private liberty. It forbade any effort to advance it by violence but proclaimed glad tidings of joy and peace.

The heavenly Author made his opinion known concerning the use of the power of government to advance his kingdom. "My kingdom is not of this world" (John 18:36). When they would have made him a king, he hid himself. When his disciples would have called fire from heaven to destroy a city, he taught them that his desire was to save and bless, not to persecute and destroy.

In the era of the apostles, Christianity was in the morning of her existence like a delightful fragrant garden, subsisting solely by the light of the Sun of Righteousness shining on all its buds, blossoms, and fruit.

Although Christianity was denied liberty, scourged from country to country for her faith and doctrines, she denied it not to others. With a heavenly simplicity she declared the glorious truth and left every individual to do with her message as they pleased, to embrace it or reject it at their own pleasure or peril.

Oh Americans, hear it! Oh you unborn millions, swear by heaven's great fire that what you were given by God you will still understand!

America has the early promise of becoming the greatest country under the sun. May millions yet unborn rise up and call this generation blessed, who, through the King of kings, secured liberty, the greatest of blessings for their posterity and the most invaluable privilege that human creatures can enjoy.

The Value of Art
John Wheelock

6

Introduction

While America clearly led the world in the political theory of freedom, our early nation was often quick to fall into imitation of Europe and Britain in the fine arts.

John Wheelock's 1774 address to Dartmouth urges students to value the arts and to recognize that the Bible contains the finest examples of poetry ever penned.

Background

Like many of America's great patriots, educators, and scholars, John Wheelock was the son of a minister. His father, Eleazar Wheelock, was a prolific participant in the Great Awakening and during John's childhood served as the "chief intelligencer of revival news" (in 1741 alone, Eleazar wrote "a hundred more sermons than there are days in the year"). The Reverend Wheelock was known all over Connecticut for his work with the revival, and he was also the director of the Moor's Indian Charity School. Eleazar often relied on his son for assistance, so it was not surprising when young John left his studies at Yale to support his father's latest project: founding Dartmouth College in Hanover, New Hampshire.

That area of New Hampshire was largely unsettled. Tracks of virgin forest separated tiny settlements and Indian villages. As part of the inaugural graduating class of 1771, John Wheelock joined a handful of other students in trying to bring higher education and the gospel of Jesus Christ to rural Americans. Yet with the advent of the Revolutionary War, young John Wheelock's life shifted from the academic to the active. He became passionately involved in local government. He organized the United Committees, groups of disgruntled New Hampshire citizens seeking more representation in the state legislature, and under his leadership twelve New Hampshire towns tried to secede from the state and join Vermont. A year later, in 1777, Wheelock briefly served in New York and Vermont as a lieutenant colonel in Colonel Bedel's Regiment. During that time he corresponded with George Washington, a man he held in the highest regard.

Wheelock's military career was cut short by the death of his father Eleazer who died in 1779, but not before recommending that his son John be appointed as president of the college. John accepted the position, despite the fact that he was neither an academic nor a minister, and held the position for almost forty years. Dartmouth prospered under Wheelock's guidance and was one of the few colleges in the nation to remain financially solvent throughout the Revolutionary War. At Wheelock's insistence, Dartmouth expanded its medical program and eventually opened the Dartmouth Medical School, which is the fourth oldest medical school in the country.

Near the end of his presidency in 1815, Wheelock wanted Dartmouth College to switch from a private school to a state-controlled institution. The board of trustees put up bitter resistance, and their argument landed the college in court. The case, *Dartmouth College v. Woodward,* was finally decided in the board's favor but not until it had traveled all the way to the United States Supreme Court (ironically, Daniel Webster, an alumnus from Dartmouth during Wheelock's tenure, argued the case on behalf of the Board). By that time Wheelock had retired from service at the college due to poor health. In 1817 he died and was buried near his father at a cemetery in Hanover, New Hampshire.

Speech

John Wheelock
Dartmouth College
1774

An Essay on the Beauties and Excellencies of Painting, Music, and Poetry

Poetry, music, and painting—of these sister arts it may be difficult to say which has created the greatest fascination for a curious mind. In every civilized nation, passionate factions of devotees for each of these forms have contended for the superiority of its favorite art. We are dazzled with the beauty and glory of these demonstrative arts. But our experience has taught us, and our reason declares that the evaluation of art involves matters of truth which ultimately must reign over personal matters of taste.

An air of apparent simplicity runs through every component of painting. Painting is a sensitive art. Is it even possible that solemn splendor or true majesty would ever be better represented than we find in Raphael's drawing of our Savior's transfiguration on the mount?

> *O! could my Fancy paint, in Strains divine,*
> *The great Raphael, in his Art sublime!*

The art of painting is surely a mark of improvement of an age.

But the more noble art of music could tame tribes most savage and rough with its soft, refined melody. With its ability to touch that which is sublime, music invigorates the soul with great and strong feelings and sentiments. It has often enraptured the minds of military forces with glowing thoughts of victory. Competing melodies of the trumpet, cornet, and the flute have emboldened army against army in the mutual clash of battle. By its power whole fields of men are convulsed, and yet they dream of conquest with ecstatic imaginations even as death beckons. The memory of the melody evokes an inner smile even as the final agony swiftly descends.

Poetry, by its effective power and energy, rules with supreme dominion over our minds. Love and hatred, joy and grief, hope and fear—all the passions are equally devoted to its sovereign power. As for music, it can only excite the social emotions. But through poetry we become interested in the deeper matters of policy and the debates of leaders executive and legislative. Poetry leads us to gain insights into the causes of war and the exploits of the brave and noble.

As for the more solid arts found in the work of the craftsman, none can deny their superior utility in common life. But the practical arts have never learned to touch the refined and secret wanderings of the soul. That which is soft, beautiful, and sublime—these, by their energy invigorate and inspire the imagination, play upon the strings of the heart, and reecho an enchanted melody. These arts of beauty reject with disdain everything uncultivated, rude and unpolished. There has never been an age, never a nation, yea I dare say an individual whose mind has not been ennobled by the cultivation of the fine arts.

Before I dismiss the subject, I would just take notice that no work of man can be compared to the poetic grandeur and sublime beauty of the sacred Scriptures. In these divine Writings, we may see the mountains weighed in scales, and the hills in a balance; we behold the caverns of the great deep laid open; we behold all nature struck with awful attention; and there we behold the heavens and the earth trembling, all emanating from the presence of the Lord! Let us view the terrors of the Almighty! We shudder with amazement and cry out with the psalmist, "Then the Earth shook and trembled, the foundations also of the hills moved, and were shaken because he was wroth. There went up a smoke out of his nostrils, and fire out of his mouth devoured; coals were kindled by it. He bowed the heavens also, and came down: and darkness was under his feet. And he rode upon a cherub and did fly: yea, he did fly upon the wings of the wind."

The Importance of Character

Josiah Stebbins

7

Introduction

In 1796, Josiah Stebbins addressed the need for steadfastness: "What ought to be done at all ought to be done well."

He cautioned graduates against two enemies of personal integrity. The first is the tendency to make moral excuses for oneself. The second is the all-too-common propensity for good people to wither in the face of scorn. Ridicule is a powerful weapon. When one lacks reason or knowledge, scoffing is a ready weapon.

Young people tend to ridicule one another in what is supposedly playful banter. I have witnessed a person with good character corrupted and destroyed by the work of a steady scoffer. Avoid such people, and do not ever make fun of or scoff at others.

Background

Like many young people of his day, Josiah Stebbins studied under his pastor before continuing on to college. Stebbins's pastor, the Reverend Nehemiah Williams, was a class of 1769 Yale graduate. He noted Stebbins's aptitude in the arena of law and recommended the boy enroll in Yale to sharpen his rhetorical skills. Stebbins not only proceeded to graduate from Yale but was also elected to the prestigious position of college tutor. For two years he spent his days keeping rowdy undergraduates in check and his nights studying law to pass the bar. By the summer of 1796, Stebbins was admitted to practice law, and although he decided to quit his position as tutor, he was asked to address the students at that year's commencement exercises. He gave a straightforward speech, opening with the words: "Common sense at once tells us that what ought to be done at all should be well done."

To some, Stebbins's next move after leaving Yale did not display much common sense. Instead of remaining in the city and opening a law practice near his distinguished friends and colleagues, Stebbins packed up his books and his bride of a few days and headed to New Milford, to "take up the burden of life in the wilderness of Maine." The law is the law whether in town or country, and Stebbins set up practice in a tiny settlement of six hundred people. He became "distinguished for his affability, his inflexible integrity, and the purity of his moral character," and eventually acquired an extensive practice and reputation.

Although far removed from the political and academic hubs of the new United States government, Stebbins did not drop out of sight or mind. In 1813 the Executive Council of Massachusetts chose him to serve as a member, and Stebbins was reelected seven years in a row. He was appointed a president elector in 1816 and was a key player in the Maine-Massachusetts Separation Convention. Stebbins was flat-out against the separation and led the opposition minority. Despite his efforts Maine split off, and Judge Stebbins's lost his seat on the bench to a pro-separation opponent. Stebbins went back to his private law practice, continuing to practice even after 1825 when he was elected (and twice reelected) to the state senate. In his typical tirelessly selfless fashion, Stebbins gave back to his community even during his senate days by serving as an overseer and trustee of Bowdoin College until his death at age sixty-three.

Speech .
Josiah Stebbins
Yale College
June 20, 1796

An Address

Common sense at once tells us that what ought to be done at all should be well done. Steadiness in our aims is essential to success. The person who bustles from object to object, from business to business, leaving each one half achieved, may as well do nothing. And we must not only pursue uniform business but pursue it unremittedly.

The heavy mind of a prejudiced person cannot move an inch toward truth, for its wheels are fast blocked and confined. Whoever attempts to convince him undertakes, as we say, a dead lift; for he can feel nothing but blows and give nothing but wounds. You cannot therefore with too much care keep your reason clear, unembarrassed, and ready to distinguish rectitude from error.

A favorite claim of many is that it is unnecessary to urge others to pursue a path of integrity. Mankind, they say, is not so inconsistent as to violate principles they feel to be just. If people only have their prejudices removed, this will induce them invariably to pursue what is right. If this were true, the greatest portion of wickedness and misery would be driven from the world. But I have no belief that the generality of mankind is better practical moralists than the man [the apostle Paul] who frankly declared, "The good that I would I do not; but the evil which I would not, that I do" (Rom. 7:19).

The mind is often led by temptation when we are fully aware that the temptation leads to error. Need I labor to prove that a greater part of the actions of people are such as they feel without a single hesitation or doubt would be wrong in others? The fact is, we deliberately do things which we know to be wrong. The lover of close bargains knows cheating is wrong, but his is a peculiar case. The malicious man knows that malice is wrong, but his is a peculiar case. In a word, every case which is one's own is a peculiar case and merely because it is one's own. Thus every man may evade every aspect of duty.

Perhaps no mortal exhibits a wider disparity comparing his professed principles with his conduct than a person of sexual impurity. Should any listener feel disposed to censure me for mentioning this sin in public, I will pause and make an apology, not for myself but for those who think an apology necessary. And it is this: those who refuse to rebuke this practice as sin have silently encouraged vices of this nature. Their silence arises from honest motives, hating to introduce into their conversation what their thoughts detested.

But there is no doubt of the duplicity of this type of sinner. Ask the debaucher whether he wishes his best-loved brother to imitate his character? Ask him whether he wishes a sister whom he loves should be connected with a man of his own character? He is struck dumb as a statue. There is no answer he can give to justify his grave inconsistency. His character and practices arise from a pretended pursuit of happiness. Yet he would shudder in horror if he thought another would seek such happiness at the expense of the virtue of his own sister. Does such a character possess integrity? Does his conduct agree with his beliefs? Are not his actions and "convictions" a contradiction? Is not his life a lie?

Many have been led away from what they know to be propriety and good sense by something which for want of a better description I shall call silly, good-natured compliance. Rather than being guided by reason, many are swayed by ridicule, which is a cheap, artificial substitute for logical reasoning. The power of ridicule has been almost incredible. A man of true ability, who knows his strength, will confront a direct opponent with a vigorous spirit, even heroism. But he may nonetheless submit with humble awe to the all-powerful laughter of a mocker. The man who boasts of his consistent principles and who supports true justice unswayed by claims of authority or counterarguments, will still shrink before sarcasm, thereby showing that generosity, friendship, truth, and religion have less control of his will than does the sneer of a fool. If we would be strong and true, we must never give way to those who practice mockery.

The aspiring politician, anxious to catch public approval, sets his reputation afloat on the sea of the noisy multitude. This teaches all his feelings to fall prostrate before the fickle god of popularity.

The public teacher, instead of directing his hearers into courses which are right, studies only how he may best encourage them in the pursuit of the paths which they have chosen; and they, being buoyed up with false hope, obediently trudge on in pursuit of error till they continue to press forward to their own destruction.

The legislator, careless to examine what laws are good, studies to draft such measures as will be pleasing to the public; forgetting that the whole business of laws is to curb men's favorite vices and that in contriving laws which shall operate without imposing restraint, he is no more rational than one who attempts to create a fire which shall burn without heat. Legislation thus becomes a farce. The lawless and disobedient become the people whose views are consulted and whose influence prevails.

Parents and instructors, either too weak out of misplaced kindness or too lazy to intervene and correct the behavior of children and their pupils, allow their minds to be overrun with such thorny sins and foolishness that they ultimately endanger their own peace, the happiness of the youths they should be training, and the welfare of society in general.

All of these are examples of those who know what is right and yet fail to do it. In this light is it even possible to question whether it is unnecessary to urge those in positions of influence to employ their offices and opportunities with integrity? No principle of behavior is more important. A person without integrity has no standard for his actions. If such a person is not eminently wicked, it is merely for lack of temptation or opportunity. When we have once violated our conscience, that ligament which binds the soul to truth, we leave our secure anchor and madly set ourselves afloat on such a broad ocean of confusion that nothing but the kind intervention of God can save us from being swallowed in its cresting waves.

Determine and fix carefully in your minds the principles which are right. Live by them punctually and inflexibly. The valley of falsehood is low ground; the descent is easy, and laziness, pleasure, and sensuality combine to urge us to glide smoothly down the long icy slope. View the danger and avoid it. Spurn sloth. Aspire to great things, and you will rise. As you become acquainted with those who pursue that which is truly great, you will obtain new vigor. You will learn to be like them; and you will give thanks to those who helped you to establish in your heart the habits of uprightness.

The Call to Patriotism   8

Paul Allen

In most colleges and universities today, patriotism is viewed as outmoded while internationalism is extolled. We are urged to unite with the world rather than uniting as a nation to secure liberty for ourselves and our posterity. American patriotism and national unity have been threatened before and must be preserved today!

Introduction

When George Washington retired from the presidency after two terms, there was a bitter electoral battle between John Adams and Thomas Jefferson in the election of 1796. Jefferson's supporters accused Adams of wanting to be a monarch, while Adams' backers accused Jefferson of being an atheist. Both of these charges were exaggerations of the respective candidate's views. Addition campaign issues involved disputes over a recent treaty with Britain and recognition of the French Revolution. Adams tended toward the British while Jefferson favored the French.

Yet, prior to the Twelfth Amendment, the runner-up for the presidency became the vice president. So in 1797, Adams was inaugurated as the second president and Jefferson became the second vice president.

On the heels of this highly divisive election, France began a series of aggressive actions toward the United States. Three French agents, who became known by the code names X, Y and Z, asked for a bribe for the French foreign minister and a significant loan for the French government in order to settle the dispute.

Our three representatives, John Marshall, Charles Pickney, and Elbridge Gerry, adamantly refused the request for the bribe and loan and revealed to the American people what had happened.

Thus, in 1797, there was a significant fear of war with France, and there were undoubtedly voices who believed it was too soon after the Revolutionary War to fight another major war.

Into the middle of this election Paul Allen, at the 1796 commencement of the College of Rhode Island, calls on America to pursue unity and patriotism.

Background

Paul Allen was born in February 1775 to a patriot father in Providence, Rhode Island, and from an early age he showed a talent for writing. After graduating from Brown University (then Rhode Island College), Allen studied for the bar but decided against a law career in favor of freelance writing. He moved from Providence to Philadelphia where he wrote for the *United Star Gazette*. Allen was fascinated by American history and geography and was thrilled to land a job editing Lewis and Clark's travel papers for the press.

Unfortunately, Allen's notoriety as a writer was short-lived. Although he was hailed for his work on the Lewis and Clark project, and was the author of a collection of miscellaneous poetry (including an epic poem on Noah's ark), Allen was unable to meet deadlines. According to Samuel Kettell's 1826 volume of *Specimens of American Poetry*, Allen struggled with debt, depression, and mental illness and was unable to complete his much-anticipated *History of the American Revolution*. However, Allen's failings later in life do not alter his perceptive comments on the need for union or benefits of patriotism during the intellectual turmoil of 1797.

Speech

Paul Allen
College of Rhode Island
July 4, 1796

An Oration on the Necessity of Political Union at the Present Day

This present age is one of wonders and an arena of revolutions. The most experienced politician, who has grown gray in the study of mankind, will find in the course of an hour all his expectations destroyed and his predictions overturned. Let us then strengthen our minds to be equal to the magnitude of the occasion, meet our misfortunes like men, and leave the rest to the disposal of providence. The force of habit and strength of education may enable us to resist this dangerous fascination with all that is new, which has already produced pictures of horror sufficient to curdle the blood in our veins.

Patriotism, which has been viewed as a noble sentiment from the birth of civilization, has been recently vilified and disgraced as being inconsistent with that liberal view which urges us to love the whole family of man from across the globe. Love of nation, it is suggested, is contrary to this innovation of thought.

But self-love is one of the strongest principles of action.

Proud of these sentiments, we cherish with reverence the image of our country's honor. The sneer of party malevolence nor the viperous tongue of slander itself can dampen the feelings of a real American.

Americans! While you justly resent the many injuries you have received from the legislators of France, remember your long and glorious struggle for independence. Great Britain, who now courts your alliance, once attempted to destroy your existence as a nation. America, young in action and unversed in the vices of Europe, has suffered much from believing the world is as generous, noble, and unprejudiced as herself. Experience, fatal experience, has yet to teach us many lessons. But whoever reads the address of the president of the United States to the federal legislature will learn that we meet our misfortunes with the reluctant spirit of a man, not the calm stupidity of an ox. It is a fact not to be denied, and it is with a mixture of pain and astonishment that I speak it, that frivolous debates—tardy and timid resolutions—have too much marked the character of our government. Europe beholds our situation, and rejoices. This vast continent may be divided into petty republics, destitute of force and energy, dangerous only to themselves, and harmless to their common enemies. But I will drive from my breast such melancholy anticipations. I will indulge the hope that there is spirit, and valor, and fortitude in our citizens, sufficient to resist this greatest of evils. Fathers! Legislators of our country! Reflect for a moment on the perilous situation of America. Is this the time for idle and unimportant debate when the world is at this crisis? Soar above the vulgar prejudices of the moment. Remain firm to your posts. Impartial posterity will do justice to your actions.

I hear the voice of our forefathers from their tombs exclaim, unite, my children, and you may yet be a happy people. Divide, and your glory, honor, and national existence are extinguished forever.

Fate wrote it with an iron pen,
And the loud thunder said Amen.

Yet if God in his wrath has ordained that this country shall fall, if discord like a colossus must stride over this continent, if all the pleasures of social life must be destroyed, if liberty, that first of heaven's blessings, must degenerate into the curse of unrestrained licentiousness, let us unite and rally round the government to a man. Let us march to the fortress of faction and expire at the mouth of the cannon. Or if driven to the walls of the sanctuary, let us embrace the pillars of the Constitution, and only in its ruins fall. Let this freeborn American hand first dig my grave in liberty and honor; and though I found but one more thus resolved, that honest man and I would die together.

Battle for Truth

Benjamin Allen

9

Introduction

In the twenty-first century, almost every student who seeks higher education will be confronted with some variant of the worldview of relativism: *There are no absolutes. There are no truths. We make our own truth. We make our own reality. The rejection of all religious truth is essential to liberty.*

Today, without anything that amounts to sufficient proof, the voices of the academy simply assert that our freedoms in general, and religious freedom in particular, arose as a consequence of the secular philosophy of Enlightenment. In my book *From Tyndale to Madison*, I review the evidence of 250 years to demonstrate that the Enlightenment had little to do with the triumph of religious liberty.

Benjamin Allen, a graduating senior from the College of Rhode Island—the one and only state to have always embraced true religious freedom—addresses the claims of secularism.

While some religions have indeed been agents of persecution, God's Word itself shows us the way to both truth and liberty.

Background

When Benjamin Allen delivered "An Oration in Defense of Divine Revelation" at Brown University, it was still the strongly Baptist Rhode Island College (renamed in 1804 after a donor, Nicholas Brown) and was known as the school that accepted scholars of diverse religious backgrounds, as opposed to the more strictly Episcopalian Columbia or Presbyterian Princeton. After Allen graduated, his speech was printed and sold in the Providence market by the local bookmakers, Carter and Wilkinson. The school had been turning out distinguished graduates since its founding in 1765, and Allen was no different.

Before he reached his forties, Allen received a professorship at New York's Union College. For several years he taught mathematics and natural philosophy to young citizens of the newest country in the New World. Fragments of letters to his son have survived, and in one of his letterbooks or journals, Allen writes descriptively of his life experiences in the months following his graduation from Rhode Island College. Some of Benjamin Allen's writings are remembered today including an 1823 Fourth of July patriotic oration, a short treatise on American education and descriptions of eighteenth-century Rhode Island life and roads.

Benjamin must have passed his love of mathematics on to his son because Horatio Allen became a famous civil engineer and operated the first locomotive in the Western Hemisphere. Due to Horatio Allen's ingenuity and direction, the West Point Foundry in New York City built the *Best Friend of Charleston*, the first locomotive produced for sale in America.

Speech

Benjamin Allen
September 6, 1797
Rhode Island College

An Oration in Defense of Divine Revelation

True religion was designed to make us kind and sociable to our fellow human beings, but religion as it is too often practiced has rendered us selfish and hard. Absurd interpretations and persecution of others have arisen from every system of religion under heaven. How often have the rights and dignity of human beings been insulted, degraded, and trampled upon? How often have the honor and character of God been violated by the misuse of his name through impure and absurd doctrines invented by the institutions of humans? How often has the sacred name of God been insulted by people acting under the feigned appearance of superior holiness? These abuses with many others committed under the mask of religious hypocrisy have caused some to reject all revelation as inconsistent with reason. This rejection of God takes improper advantage of common people and in the end is an insult to mankind—created in the image of the true God—and an even more profound insult to the character of the Almighty.

Those who exalt reason as the enemy of all revelation artfully imply or openly declare that the true religion from our Savior stands on the same foundation with that from Mohammed and the fables of antiquity. They insist that all theories of the divine arise from ignorance and that all are equally a false imposition on mankind. They renounce all the forms of enlightenment that come from the claims of divine revelation; they place their trust in the forlorn "age of reason." They aim their wit and ridicule at Christianity and treat with unholy and ungenerous contempt the life of the Son and his immortality which brought true light to the world through the gospel.

They add insult to the misfortunes of life. They scoff at the beauties of our promised heavenly paradise, changing the view of the hereafter into the barren land of nonexistence.

As we lower our loved ones into the grave, their scoffing supplants our hope for eternity with the seeds of annihilation. They equate humans with beasts. We are destined, they say, to be like a meteor of the night, blazing for a moment then vanishing forever into shades of darkness.

Let us not give way to such skeptics and thereby deprive others of that one true religion which alone can alleviate the misfortunes of life.

In these days we have rejoiced with all those who seek the legal toleration and freedom of all religious opinion. But some with whom we have joined in supporting liberty have turned their eloquent pens and minds to oppose all revelation. They have in some instances captivated the passions and seduced the judgment of those who listen. They have with unrestrained glee attacked the character of the clergy. We are aware that some have abused their ministerial offices; they are rightfully exposed to all. But let us not indiscriminately attack a group of people who have been so important and useful to mankind. Any improved society cannot exist without them. They help form the mind and mend the heart.

But what have the systems and errors of men to do with the religion of heaven? We renounce all systems but the system of God. Some, in supporting their favorite opinions, have undoubtedly been led into error. Human error does not detract from God's truth.

While we smile at the incomprehensible commentaries written by those who seek to create theological systems, our deep admiration for the great original [the Bible] is increased. Like its divine author, it cannot be destroyed. Heaven and earth shall pass away, and nature will dissolve at the feet of God, but true religion exists forever.

As a system coming from heaven, with evidence of its divine inspiration marked on every page, the revealed Word ought to influence our belief and actions. But, some say, belief in the Christian Scriptures is no proof of their truth or importance. Because, continue the objectors, the same proof is applicable to every system of error extant. Belief in that which is false does not make it true. Disbelief of the truth does not make it false. This will be granted. Things are either true or false, independent of belief. "Man cannot create; he can only discover."

But the mere fact that some believe in false systems of religion is no proof that the only system of religion which exhibits the obvious evidence of God's handiwork is also false. Virtue is never more self-evident than when contrasted with vice. To reject all truth merely because we are liable to err is the height of absurdity.

The weakness of human reason to determine many things in morals and religion points out to us the necessity of some superior guide, of some unerring standard to which we may refer our actions and appreciate their worth. The very idea of man's moral agency involves in it the supposition of laws to ascertain and govern his actions. From whom can those originate but the Legislator of the universe? If God governs the natural world by universal laws, why not the moral? The same necessity is evident in both. The promulgation of these laws is the revelation that we plead for. The necessity and importance of such a revelation becomes a serious and all-interesting enquiry. It involves in it our present and future happiness.

The great goal that God had in mind, delivering to mankind a transcript of his mind, was to make known to us God's true character. He sought to teach us by what our real happiness consists; to confirm the wishes of our hearts in immortality; to offer the greatest incentives to virtue, the greatest deterrents from vice, by establishing the doctrine of a future state of rewards and punishments. Some parts of God's revealed Word seem too difficult for us to fully grasp, even incomprehensible at times. Our inability to comprehend fully has been seized upon by skeptics who loudly and boldly argue that this incomprehensibility decisively proves that the entire text lacks veracity.

If we are to reject as untrue that which we cannot fully comprehend, we should then reject the truth of our own existence because we cannot fully comprehend the laws that govern our human bodies. Shall we disbelieve the existence of all those scenes of creation because we cannot comprehend *all* the laws by which they are governed? Mankind, after all our wonderful discoveries, will find more to admire than to comprehend—more to animate our devotion than to confirm our unbelief.

This, so far from being an effective argument against the truth of revelation, is one of the greatest in its favor. If man had been the Bible's author, would it not in every respect have been within the sphere of man's comprehension? Like all the works of man, whether of genius or imitation, it might have been perfectly understood.

Omniscience is an attribute of God only. It is sufficient for us that we can learn our duty and powerful enough to prompt us to performance. Revelation teaches both lessons with unmistakable clarity. All knowledge flows from God. The mind that can fully comprehend the anatomy of a fly is equal to the knowledge of the universe. The power that can give animation to a mite can with the same ease move unnumbered worlds.

Astonished at the wonderful discoveries made in philosophy, some have supposed divine revelation to be superfluous. But however extensive man's knowledge may be, however he may have improved his mind or exalted his nature through reason and philosophy, at the end of all his deliberations, we find only uncertainty. On his own man has no explanation for what happens at the end of physical life.

Clouds and darkness hover over the regions of the grave. We see man's entrance into life; we observe the development of his mind and reasoning in all his wonderful discoveries; we follow him to the tomb, but without the light of divine revelation, at the tomb we lose man forever.

The love of God for man, in pardoning his sins and

restoring him to future happiness, can never be discovered by the efforts of human reason, no matter how brilliant the philosopher.

The human mind, long before the dawn of the Christian era, had arrived at an astonishing degree of refinement. Poetry was sublime, oratory astonishingly eloquent, and philosophy had traced the principles of morality. But the great problem of man's immortality remained unsolved. It was reserved for divine revelation to demonstrate the truth of man's resurrection. God's revealed voice awakes the slumbers of the tombs and renders man a new creation. He proclaims the redeemed to be heirs of immortal glory—a bright train of saints who bow before the blazing throne of God.

The Folly of Intellectualism

Timothy Dwight

10

Introduction

Harvard and Yale were both founded as orthodox Christian schools. Why did they lose their way? When did they lose their way? Timothy Dwight, president of Yale, in this 1797 speech to the students, believed that some of these tendencies had already found their way into the student body. He vigorously addressed these issues during his tenure at Yale.

Using the Bible as the ultimate source of truth, Dwight closely examined the propensity of students toward intellectual pride. When individuals or institutions love knowledge of men more than they love God's Word, the seeds of deceit are injected into the soil, waiting to spring forth as a crop of lies and folly.

Background

Perhaps you would not expect the Yale of the 1790s to bear any resemblance to the Yale of the 1960s, but there were similarities. Post-Revolutionary War ideas of enlightenment and equality were causing students to protest authority in its various forms, from dress code to curfew to class materials. When President Ezra Stiles died in 1795, Timothy Dwight became head of an establishment where "intemperance, profanity, and gambling were common; yea, and also licentiousness." The works of Tom Paine were cultishly popular, spawning deistic societies among students eager to lecture their elders on the indomitableness of the human spirit and the supremacy of human reason in all things.

When forty-three-year-old Dwight returned to his alma mater, he was not pleased at the relaxed atmosphere of the school in regards to academic discipline. Dwight had received his B.A. from Yale in 1776, and when he became president twenty years later, he proceeded to reinstitute the schedule he remembered from his own dorm days. This included a 5:30 a.m. start to the day, facilitated by the ringing of a large bell. Once the students were up, they were expected to trek, regardless of weather, to an outbuilding washhouse, and arrive clean and composed for Dwight's 6:00 a.m. chapel. As the building was not equipped with a furnace, Dwight often preached facing the baleful stares of shivering students. After chapel was an hour of student recitations, presented from material crammed in the night before. At 8:00 a.m. the students breakfasted on coffee, toast, and the occasional dish of bay oysters and then hit the books to prepare for their 11:00 a.m. recitations. Students usually had free time from 1:00 p.m. to 4:00 p.m., with the chance of more recitations in that window. Vigilant tutors lurked outside student's rooms during study periods, hoping to surprise illegal nap-takers. At 6:00 p.m. President Dwight led a prayer service prior to supper, but that left students a whole hour of free time before the 9:00 p.m. curfew. They were free to explore the city and surrounding countryside during that hour as long as they were already prepared for the next morning's recitations. As one frazzled student reported home: "Our lessons are sufficient to employ the greatest part of the class from 6 o'clock in the morning till 9 o'clock at night; excepting the time taken up by prayers, meals, and recitations, and perhaps two hours during the day for recreation."

However, Dwight wanted method in his madness. He did away with Ezra Stiles's compulsory study and practice of Hebrew because he quickly realized that few students were interested in reading the Bible. They blatantly mocked the Yale creed, which said, "If any Scholar shall deny the Holy Scriptures . . . to be of divine authority; or shall . . . endeavor to propagate among the Students any error or heresy subverting the foundations of the Christian religion, and shall persist therein, after admonition, he shall be dismissed." Dwight noticed groups of young men calling each other by "enlightened" nick-names, such as Voltaire, and was disgusted. Apparently, the grandson of Jonathan Edwards had inherited a school of 110 hostile students, most of whom described themselves as skeptics.

Dwight immediately began contrasting their liberal philosophies against his own biblical beliefs and challenged them to scrutinize the effects their philosophies were having on people living in Europe. Dwight introduced oratory as a study and promoted the study and mastery of the English language in addition to Hebrew. Initially, his students were horrified at his infatuation with Bible stories and constant praises for the lyric texts found in Scripture, but Dwight had settled in to stay.

In addition to acting as president, Dwight taught as Yale's professor of divinity, and his classroom became a jousting field. He pounded his students with questions on current events and issues: What did they believe about just war theory, capital punishment, foreign immigration, or religious liberty? Departing from the stiff, formal lecture-style system Ezra Stiles had instituted, Dwight made his undergraduates grapple with their own unanswered questions. Some of them included: Is a lie ever justifiable? Should Christianity be required for government office? Is man living in a perfectible state? Dwight found that his group of hostile skeptics were really just unmoored teenagers seeking to make sense of their changing world.

However, Dwight believed in absolutes and that they

had a Source. A few months into his tenure, Dwight told the seniors to submit written questions on any controversial subject they wanted to hear him tackle. Although, per Yale's creed, such a question was illegal, a senior submitted the following query: "Are the Scriptures of the Old and New Testament the word of God?"

Intrigued, Dwight polled his class and was taken aback at their response: every senior said no, Scripture is not God breathed. He asked them to defend their answer, and each explained the Bible was riddled with flaws. Drawing on his extensive knowledge of Scripture, Dwight responded by critiquing their arguments and examining the weaknesses of the deistic argument. Six months later in student chapel, Dwight was still lecturing on the Divine authority of Scripture. In an earnest effort to educate his skeptics, Dwight worked extra hours and gave additional lectures on Evidences of Divine Revelation.

By 1796 only one freshman was a Christian, none of the sophomores were, and only one of the juniors would confess Christ. However, in Dwight's senior class there were eight to ten Bible-believing Christians. Dwight continued preaching and teaching, and within seven years Yale experienced revival. Of 230 young men, one third converted, and thirty of those new Christians immediately pursued public ministry. "Dwight, through the blessing of God, changed the college from a sink of moral and spiritual pollution into a residence not only of science and literature but of morality and religion, a nursery of piety and virtue, a fountain whence has issued streams to make glad the city of God," wrote one graduate.

As the son of a Christian Federalist soldier who had served under General Washington, Dwight's earliest playmates were sound doctrine and fervent patriotism. He kept tabs on the events leading up to the French Revolution and paid special attention to the bloody years of 1797–1800. Mixed into his patriotic soul was a strong poetic streak; he wrote stanza upon stanza of love poetry to the Land of the Brave.

From age seventeen onwards Dwight supported himself, first by teaching at the Hopkins Grammar School at New Haven, and then tutoring at Yale from 1771 to 1777. By the time he was eighteen, Dwight was known as an outspoken critic of radical republicanism and "infidel philosophy." He fearlessly condemned the philosophies of Hume, Hobbes, Tindal, and Lords Shaftesbury and Bolingbroke; and his address to the candidates for the baccalaureate in Yale College was published in book form and is credited as one of the embers of the Second Great Awakening.

In his free time he studied Newton's *Principia*, read law books, and served two terms in the Massachusetts legislature. He almost accepted a nomination for Congress, but at that point Dwight realized his vocational calling was behind a pulpit. In 1783, at age thirty-one, Dwight became the pastor of Greenfield Hill, where he preached until moving to Yale in 1795. Dwight's *Theology Explained and Defended* is an impressive compilation of 173 sermons, and he is also numbered among the great American hymn writers for his adaptations of thirty-three of David's psalms.

For nearly forty-six years of his life, Dwight selflessly taught his fellow Americans about the Source of order and the Author of liberty. Twenty-two classes graduated from Yale during his presidency, and at his death the college had doubled in size and more than trebled in prestige.

Influence/Audience: Henry Baldwin, Lyman Beecher, Benjamin Silliman

In 1797 when Timothy Dwight warned the young men against following philosophies "after the tradition of men," he was speaking to a future justices, preachers, inventors, and legislators. Sitting in the audience (or more likely, standing) in the crowded Yale chapel was seventeen-year-old Henry Baldwin, the Connecticut-born law student and journalist who would later serve fourteen years as a justice on the U.S. Supreme Court during the turbulent presidency of Andrew Jackson. Henry Baldwin was twice reelected to the House of Representatives where he served as chairman of the House Committee on Domestic Manufactures. During the War of 1812, he was elected to the Pittsburgh City Public Safety Council, but it is for his work on the High Court that Justice Baldwin is remembered.

Baldwin was radically opposed to slavery, and one wonders if Dwight's classroom lectures on the justice inherent in God's character were a seed that led to Baldwin's outspoken defense of freedom. Stiles, Dwight's predecessor, had been a slave owner[4] while simultaneously acting as president of The Connecticut Society for the Promotion of Freedom and for the Relief of Persons Unlawfully Holden in Bondage, a state of affairs that Baldwin found disgusting. Slavery to Baldwin was plain evil. In one case, that of *Johnson v. Tompkins*,[5] Baldwin instructed the jury that while slavery was legal, they should keep in mind that its existence "is abhorrent to all our ideas of natural right and justice," and that was not an isolated incident.

However, the American judicial process is a complicated beast, and on one occasion Baldwin found himself voting against freedom. He was the sole dissenter in the 1840 Amistad Case in which the Court decided to free a ship of illegally imported African slaves. Baldwin hated slavery, but he voted against freeing the slaves because he feared an increase of federal interference in private trade practices. Government needed limitations.

Earlier, in 1831, Baldwin had actually considered resigning from the Supreme Court because of its power-hungry tendencies. In a letter to President Jackson, Baldwin complained about the court's extension of powers. Jackson, wrote Baldwin, might not be fully aware that such abuse of power inevitably leads to the misinterpretation of the Constitution. Yet although he was indignant, Baldwin did not resign. Instead he authored an 1837 treatise titled *A*

General View of the Origin and Nature of the Constitution and Government of the United States: Deduced from the Political History and Condition of the Colonies and States, excerpts of which are still read today.

Baldwin's eloquence and morality throughout his life are a tribute to the quality of early America's college education system. During that same graduation ceremony, it is possible that a few pews over from the about-to-graduate Baldwin sat another eminent American, Lyman Beecher. Beecher, who would play an important role in the Second Great Awakening, had come to Yale strictly to pursue his divinity studies under Dwight.

Beecher remembered Dwight's presence as "singularly commanding, enforced by a manner somewhat authoritative and emphatic," and strove to emulate the president's "clear, hearty, and sympathetic" way of speaking. Dwight had a voice, according to Beecher, which entered "into the soul like the middle notes of an organ," and Dwight often employed it to exhort his students out of his vast knowledge of philosophy, science, Scripture, and language. In addition to all his other virtues, writes one contemporary, Dwight was personable. "His smile was irresistible."

After completing intensive theological studies with Dwight, Lyman Beecher was ordained in 1799 as a Presbyterian clergyman. He moved to Long Island and began to build his reputation as a preacher, political commentator, and teetotaler. He was not afraid to address his congregation on current events and did not shrink from controversy. In one sermon, well over two hours long, Beecher recounted the duel between Hamilton and Burr. That sermon, strongly Calvinistic, gained him popularity in 1806; and Beecher began printing and distributing his weekly sermons, most of which warned against Unitarianistic teachings.

Lyman Beecher had many remarkable and famous children, including Harriet Beecher Stowe, Henry Ward Beecher, Charles Beecher, Edward Beecher, Isabella Beecher Hooker, and Catharine Beecher. As their homeschool dad and primary educator, Beecher probably gave his children Timothy Dwight's compiled sermons as assigned reading, including Dwight's address to Yale titled, "On the Nature and Dangers of Infidel Philosophy."

On another pew, probably nearer the back, sat another of Dwight's talented pupils, eighteen-year-old Benjamin Silliman. The boy was enthusiastic about law, but Dwight had other plans for Silliman and appointed him as Yale's first professor of chemistry and natural history. Dwight's choice seems puzzling in light of the fact that Silliman had virtually zero knowledge of chemistry. However, Dwight chose him for his character and for the potential Dwight saw in him. That potential did not disappoint.

In 1802 Dwight insisted that Silliman attend the University of Pennsylvania's medical school. After two years of intense study and practice, Silliman returned to Yale and founded Yale's Medical Institution. He taught at both the college and the medical school and is remembered for setting up elaborate classroom demonstrations that often amazed the students. Silliman's course was said to be one of the high points in the Yale medical curriculum, and Dwight deserves partial credit for Silliman's success.

It is remarkable to think that Dwight's involvement in the life of one young student led to the founding of Yale's Medical Institution and untold numbers of medical discoveries. Silliman eventually acquired an international reputation as a chemist and author. He was also the founder and editor of the *American Journal of Science*.

Speech

Timothy Dwight
Yale College
September 9, 1797

The Nature and Danger of Infidel Philosophy, Exhibited in Two Discourses

"Beware lest any man spoil you through philosophy and vain deceit, after the tradition of men, after the rudiments of the world, and not after Christ."

—Colossians 2:8

When the gospel was published by the apostles, it was vigorously opposed by the world. This opposition originated from various sources; but wherever it appeared, it wore one uniform character of structure, design, and bitterness. The opposition of the Jews, the sword of the Gentiles, the learning of the wise, the persuasion of the eloquent, and the force of the powerful were alike exerted to crush the rising enemy: the gospel.

Among these forces of opposition, which the apostles were called to encounter was the philosophy of the age. A large number of their first converts lived in countries where the language of the Greeks was spoken and the Greek philosophy received. The things which this philosophy professed to teach were substantially the same subjects taught by the apostles. Greek philosophy assumed the position of a rival to the gospel. It was an imposing force, especially on the young and unsettled converts.

The doctrines and the spirit of the philosophers were generally direct counterparts to those of the apostles. Some truths, and truths of high importance, they undoubtedly taught; but they blended them with gross and numberless errors. Some moral and commendable practices they inculcated, but they were so interwoven with immoralities that the parts of the web could never be separated by the common hand. Covetous, self-sufficient, and sensual, they looked down with supreme contempt on the poor, self-denying, and humble followers of Christ and on their unsophisticated, direct, undistinguished, and practical preaching. Their philosophy was enveloped in fable and figures, riddled with sophistry, never coming to an end but constantly wandering in perpetual motion around moral subjects. It could never give permanent satisfaction to the mind or useful conclusions for the heart, while the gospel, with its simple, plain, and powerful message, was ratified by the common sense of the listener, impacting mind, soul, and emotions. Of course, the contempt for the gospel held by the philosophers changed into hatred, rivalry, and persecution. They began with ridicule of Christianity but proceeded to serious efforts of violence and hatred.

In Colossians 2:8 this philosophy is characterized in a most proper and forcible manner. It is deceitful in its nature, doctrines, and arguments and vain in its efficacy to accomplish the ends which it proposes. Paul makes clear that it comes from *the tradition of men*, and *after the rudiments of the world*; but *not after Christ*; *in whom*, the apostle notes, *dwelt all the fullness of the Godhead bodily*.

Philosophy is a scheme that is perfectly suited to the character of its inventors: men who are weak and wicked, deceived and deceitful; unable to devise, to comprehend, or to teach, the character of God or the duty of mankind. It is such a scheme of morals and religion and reflects the principles and practices of the disciples of this philosophy. It taught not with a design to amend the heart and reform the life but with a view to gain acceptance by flattering man's lust and by justifying, soothing, and quieting guilt. It is equally remote from truth, equally unsupported by evidence, and equally fraught with danger and ruin.

I feel it, young gentlemen, to by my duty, on this occasion, to exhort you to beware lest you become prey to the philosophy which opposes the gospel. They reason like this: Bread, we know, will nourish a man and safely determine that bread was formed for this end. But why man exists at all, why he thus exists, and why he is thus to be nourished, we know not. For we can only conjecture whether man will exist beyond the grave.

The explanations for the purposes of man's life offered by philosophy are no better than the explanations offered by a clown concerning the intricate designs of a statesman in the management of a great empire. A clown's observations do not enable the statesman to determine his future course, nor do they enlighten any aspect of his duty or the duties of his fellow subjects. Yet the clown is infinitely nearer to the statesman in understanding than the philosopher is to the Supreme Ruler.

Man is not only a subject of the divine government, needing to know and obey the divine law, but he is also a subject who is in rebellion. He, therefore, must make it his highest concern to discover the means of being restored to the favor of God. Man has violated the teachings of divine law, which are knowable either by revelation or common sense. He should have discovered and should acknowledge God's precepts that require him to be sincere, just, and kind to his fellowmen.

Those philosophers who acknowledge God generally agree that such precepts are the plain duties of man. Could we then discover the law of God by examining his works, the knowledge of it would avail nothing to our future well-being. That we are sinners cannot be disputed; and, so far as philosophy can discover, sinners must be condemned and punished.

The true character of all men may be certainly known by their opinions. No man is better than the moral opinions he holds. Few live up to their professed opinions, but none live on a higher plane than that which they profess.

A Discourse on Liberty
David Tappan

11

Introduction

Religious liberty was still a new concept as the eighteenth century was drawing to a close in America. Government no longer claimed the power to coerce men to believe religious doctrines of its choice—at least in America.

With this newfound freedom a dangerous tendency developed to cast off all restraint in the name of liberty.

David Tappan, president of Harvard, struck the right balance in a 1798 graduation at that institution. Government cannot legitimately control our consciences, but Almighty God has full jurisdiction to judge our thoughts, beliefs, and actions. True liberty recognizes the rule of God in our hearts and minds.

Background

After applying himself extensively to academics, fourteen-year-old David Tappan enrolled at Harvard University. His classmates remember a student "distinguished in propriety of conduct," diligent and successful in his studies—until he fell gravely ill. During his third year at Harvard, Tappan caught a virus that nearly killed him. The vibrant young man found himself trapped in bed, weak and almost completely helpless. Instead of wallowing in self-pity and disappointed hopes, Tappan devoted himself to reading. But he didn't read Homer or Aristotle; rather, the writings of the apostles and prophets. He devoured both the Old and New Testaments, reading them again and again. As the words of Christ and the prophets took hold in his heart, Tappan became more and more concerned with the state of his soul. A concern for his spiritual education replaced his hunger for a secular one. As soon as he received his B.A. in 1771, Tappan immediately dove into a comprehensive study of theology; for two solid years he did little else except read, memorize, and write about the Bible as well as weighing and analyzing what others had written on its texts.

By age twenty-one Tappan had a reputation as a scholar and was pastoring a sizable church in Newbury, Massachusetts; and his circle of influence was widening. His sermons were published and circulated throughout the colonies, much to his embarrassment. At first, when friends wanted to publish his ordination sermons, Tappan had refused to allow them to go to press. After much urging, he finally yielded.

The community knew Tappan as a man of irreproachable character and found that "his first efforts in the pulpit evinced an uncommonly mature mind, and an extent of theological attainment which would have done no discredit to venerable age." He became quite popular. During the 1800s, David Tappan was among the most widely printed clergyman in North America. By the time Harvard asked him to fill the office of professor of divinity, Tappan was considered a prime candidate. He had been pastoring the Newbury Church for almost eighteen years and was reluctant to leave it. However, an ecclesiastical council was called, and the church as a whole decided that God was calling Tappan back to Harvard. Tappan preached a farewell sermon of "melting tenderness," packed up with his wife Hannah and their numerous children, and moved back to Cambridge and the small, provincial institution that had been so instrumental in shaping his own life.

By 1798 Tappan had tremendous influence with both the undergraduates and the surrounding community. When he preached, and he often officiated at funerals and other occasions, the churches and meetinghouses packed out. Four years previously Harvard had made Tappan a doctor of divinity, and he was one of the most popular preachers in Massachusetts.

On an August Sunday in 1803, Tappan traveled to a

neighboring church to preach and returned in a state of utter exhaustion. He lay down on his bed and died a mere twenty days later. During his illness Tappan remarked, "The doctrines of grace which contemplate men as sinners, and as requiring an infinite atonement, are the doctrines which I must live and die by." A few hours before he died, Tappan said his hope was on "the cornerstone laid in Zion, elect and precious. If I do not trust there, I know not in what I do trust. I have nothing else to trust in. Lord, to whom shall I go? Thou hast the words of eternal life!" An observer at Tappan's bedside said that "his spirit departed" while he was in the act of praying, his head tilted back and his eyes straining toward heaven.

Speech

David Tappan
Harvard College
June 19, 1798

A Discourse

The present crisis of human affairs is solemn and momentous. And it would seem that this university is soon to send a considerable number of her sons to the service of their country and mankind. I cannot but seize this significant opportunity to address them and the students at large with some observations and counsels, suggested chiefly by the present state of the world.

These counsels may be appropriately introduced by the timely advice of Solomon to young persons in Proverbs 19:27, "Cease, my son, to hear the instruction that causeth to err from the words of knowledge."

This inspired and parental caution is plainly intended to guard the rising generation against those wrong and dangerous opinions that would seduce them from the principles and practice of sound morality and piety; whether such opinions be earnestly taught by philosophers, artfully insinuated by wits, or powerfully enforced by political reformers; whether they be privately uttered in social circles or propagated like a general pestilence in lewd publications.

I shall mention the dangerous but all too fashionable contention that philosophical principles are equally innocent. This arises from the application of the unalienable right of private judgment—that is, the liberty of thinking as we please on every subject; our moral responsibility does not extend to regulate our thoughts but to our actions only. Human conduct is influenced, not by what we think, but by emotions and natural inclinations, that a person who happens to fall into error, may be as honest and virtuous as one who embraces truth, and consequently, that if the Christian religion should prove to be true, a man may be as sincere in not believing as in assenting to it.

We shall not oppose these false ideas which flatter man's

ego by opposing or in the least disparaging the principle of the inalienable liberty of thought. Liberty of conscience is the boast of our enlightened and liberal age. We admit, yea, earnestly contend that every man is both entitled and bound to examine and judge for himself upon every important question and that he need not answer for his opinions to any tribunal on earth. But does it follow that he is not accountable to God and his own conscience for the manner in which he conducts himself?

Is not the connection between the head and the heart, between judgment and practice, intimate and strong? Do not evil tendencies, indulgent behavior, and prejudices often mislead our minds into embracing licentious opinions? In a word, are not an unbelieving mind and the practice of infidelity alternate causes and effects of each other? A man with a wicked heart and life eagerly resorts to irreligious principles to justify himself; do not such principles, in return, directly encourage and patronize wickedness?

The great distinction between good and wicked men lies in this, that the former, though they may hold some philosophical errors, are for the most part governed not by these mistakes but by those important truths which they usually and fondly embrace; the latter, while they may agree with some truths of real significance, in practice they disregard these truths, and in their prevailing opinions and conduct they hold to and are molded by falsehood.

The man who sets aside the great truths on which

virtue rests, such as the being, character, or government of God; the desirability and obligation of holiness, justice, sincerity, temperance, and chastity; the man who rejects all moral distinctions and teaches the appropriateness of lying, fraud, cruelty, lewdness, and irreligion; such a man cannot be of virtuous character. His principles directly operate to extinguish every virtuous sentiment, feeling, and action and to nourish every opposite quality. It is incredible that an honest and good heart should embrace, much less eagerly propagate such errors. It is equally unlikely that such principles should fail to undermine the morals, the minds, and the conduct of those who zealously promote such ideas. "He who is pleased with error is a friend to vice and a destroyer of his own well-being as well as a dishonorer of the God of truth."

Deists claim that their disbelief of Christianity is sincere and they mean no harm by it; yet their rejection of God reveals a spirit of moral depravity that is both substantial and real. While a spirit of humility and integrity, of devotion and charity has, in numberless instances, led to or been unspeakably improved by the belief of Christianity, it is a fact that the lives of the greater part of infidels have been unfriendly both to virtue and holiness. Most deistic writers have fought to undermine natural religion and morality as well as the Christian faith. If they really and practically believed their own doctrines, how depraved must have been their moral characters!

We appeal to common sense and ask, "Is there not an

essential difference in the character and ruling principles of a Washington and a Robespierre, of the present president of our country and that of a certain great and terrible republic?" While you are struck with the contrast between these several characters, do you not feel a sacred obligation to copy the integrity, the patriotism, the active philanthropy of the one and to avoid the selfishness, injustice, and villainy of the other?

Behold France converted into one great theater of falsehood and perjury, of cruelty and ferocity, of robbery and piracy, of anarchy and despotism, of fornication and adultery, and of course reduced to a state of unspeakable degradation and misery. Compare this picture with the existing character and state of our own country with the unsullied purity of its public administration and the general order, refinement, and happiness of its citizens; and then say, "Which is the most friendly to the human character and condition, the atheistical system of France or the Christian institutions of America?" Does not the comparison force a conviction?

I entreat you to carry these moral sentiments along with you into the future scenes of active life. Never forget that sound philosophy, as well as Christianity, teaches that you were made not for yourselves only but for God and the universe; that you were intended to serve not merely the purposes of time but those of eternity. Beseech the Author of your frame to impress these ideas on your minds, to inspire your hearts with corresponding convictions, and thus to form in you a generous and elevated character, becoming reasonable, social, and immortal beings.

The most ardent and anxious friendship cannot wish you a greater good than that after a long scene of honorable and useful conduct founded on pious and evangelical principles, Christianity may "seat herself by your dying pillows, draw aside the curtains of eternity, point your closing eyes to the opening gates" of everlasting life, and convey your departing spirits in peace and transport to a state of perfect, ever-growing knowledge, virtue, enjoyment, usefulness, and glory.

Attack on Atheism

Jonathan Maxcy

12

Introduction

At the beginning of the twenty-first century, we have seen a renewed attack by outspoken atheists whose public denunciations of the existence of God have been given prominence in the secular media.

Today's secular atheists claim that their philosophy is the road to freedom and the future of mankind. They attempt to wrap themselves in the mantle of the American founders with the pretense that America was founded on secularist notions.

President Jonathan Maxcy of Rhode Island College addresses the forces of atheism that were present in his day. Atheism was the guiding principle of the French Revolution.

Maxcy lays out the convincing case on the necessity of

believing in God, the immortality of the soul of man, and the necessary connection between God and public morality.

The second prong is especially worthy of note. If any one religious principle was considered the most important in early America, it was the necessity of believing in an eternal soul.

The founders knew that power was dangerous and the temptations facing those in power were significant. It was the belief that God would judge the immortal soul of man that served as a check and balance upon this propensity to selfishness and evil. Belief in the doctrine of eternal rewards and punishments was widely acknowledged as an essential character qualification for public leadership.

It is good to remind ourselves today that we serve a God who will judge all.

Background

The precocious, eloquent, and outrageously youthful American scholar Jonathan Maxcy became the second president of Rhode Island College (now Brown University) at an age which modern American twenty-somethings find incredible. Although he was formally elected president in 1797, Maxcy began acting as president *pro tempore* at age twenty-four. At the commencement ceremonies after Maxcy was named president *pro tempore*, an indignant student put a sign in the attic window of College Hall emblazoned with Maxcy's name above the words, "President 24 years old."

Remarkably, Maxcy actually had the necessary experience to make a good college president. He had been leading services and delivering sermons at Providence's First Baptist Church for some time, and was on the college's board of trustees. A colleague and professor at the college, Professor Romeo Elton, recalled: "The University over which he [Maxcy] presided [provided] distinguished honor to himself and benefit to the public, and flourished under his administration. His fame was extended over every section of the Union."

The newly United States experienced rapid growth in the founding of institutions of higher learning, and in 1802 Maxcy resigned his post at Brown to become president of Union College in Schenectady, New York (where he succeeded the prolific Reverend Jonathan Edwards). Two years later Maxcy left New York in search of a more healthful climate, eventually settling in South Carolina where he became the extremely popular president of South Carolina College. He died in Columbia on June 4, 1820.

During his tenure at Brown, Maxcy inspired a number of high-achieving Americans, including the young firebrand Tristam Burges; John Holmes, a future congressman and senator from Maine; James Tallmadge, a future member of congress from New York and also lieutenant governor; Jeremiah Chaplin, the future president of Waterville College; Nathan F. Dixon, a future senator from Rhode Island; Andrew Pickens, future governor of South Carolina; Henry Wheaton, future U.S. ambassador and author of the internationally acclaimed book *Elements of International Law*; and Samuel W. Bridgham, who would become the first mayor of Providence.

Speech

Jonathan Maxcy
Rhode Island College
September 5, 1798

An Address

You, gentlemen, have the unique fortune to complete the course of your collegiate education at a period the most alarming and interesting the world ever saw. Principles and conduct prevail which threaten destruction of those institutions of religion and government to which mankind is indebted for all the blessings of civilized life. In that part of Europe passions have suddenly boiled to a level of such uncontrolled rage that they have defied the sacred obligations of religion and justice, have proclaimed open war against the Almighty, and have covered the earth with blood and murder. There you behold tigers and wolves in human form sparing neither age nor sex. To them a supreme being is a despicable monster; immortality is unconscious sleep; and any thoughts that there they may face eternal consequences for their action is to them nothing more than the offspring of superstition.

There in Europe the monster of despotism riding on her iron chariot gnashes her bloody jaws and growls threats of destruction to the whole world. From this horrid spectacle turn your eyes to your native country where laws are regarded, where government is equally administered, where the constituted authorities are respected, where the God of heaven is worshipped; and let your full souls rise with an solemn determination to resist at all events the intruding arm of foreign domination.

When you see the patently harmful effects of infidelity, atheism, and unbridled ambition, learn to honor and support those sacred institutions which alone can render men fit subjects for moral and civil government.

Remember, there is a God.

The belief of this truth is the only security of virtue and the only barrier against vice. For if we say there is no God, we say there is no standard of morality. We equalize virtue with vice, or rather we say there are no such things as virtue and vice. We at once annihilate all moral obligation and with it all restraint on the sinful propensities and headstrong passions of man. It is truly astonishing that a rational being who is capable of even a moment of reflection should be an atheist, and yet many spurn at the idea of God and arrogantly tell you that the universe is not an effect but a cause.

Indeed, if you disbelieve the existence of God, you must believe there is not a higher principle than matter. Accordingly, you must say matter is eternal and its various forms, animate and inanimate, are the result of some random power.

If this is your view, you will gain nothing and will lose much. You will still be at a loss for whatever power you have created in your own theory for the existence of matter just as you are unable to account for the existence of God—who is eternal, intelligent, and uncaused.

If you admit the existence of God, you can account for the origin of all things in a consistent manner; if you believe that some random power or process created matter, you can never account for the existence of one atom or for one modification of matter.

Atheism is of all doctrines the most uncomfortable and gloomy. It renders all moral and intellectual acquirements useless; lowers man to the level of a mere brute; destroys all order, design, and harmony in the universe. If acted out in its genuine effects, it would convert the world into a theater of confusion, violence, and misery. Never, therefore, forget there is a God. Let every breath you draw, every object you behold, remind you of this truth.

Remember that you have souls and that these will never cease to exist. A denial of the existence of the soul as a thing distinct from matter, and of its immortality is a natural and necessary consequence of a denial of the existence of God. In this view the state of man and brutes is the same. Both are matter, and both are destroyed by decomposition. In short, the doctrine of a material soul amounts to this, man has no soul.

God has so formed you that you are obliged to rely on your common sense to evaluate truth. If you distrust the evidence that your senses plainly recognize, you have no standard of certainty left. Just as your eyes see the mountains, your inner senses recognize the existence of your souls. To doubt therefore whether you have souls is to doubt whether anything exists.

God's revealed Word alone assures and confirms immortality for man. In the sacred pages a distinction is clearly made and kept up between the body and the soul. God is styled "the God of spirit and of flesh." Paul speaks of "the spirits of just men made perfect" (Heb. 12:23). Job says, "There is a spirit in man" (Job 32:8). David says, "Into thine hand I commit my spirit" (Ps. 31:5). Christ said to his disciples, "A spirit hath not flesh and bones" (Luke 24:39). Stephen, when stoned to death, cried, "Lord Jesus, receive my spirit" (Acts 7:59). The Savior certainly taught there was a difference between spirit and matter when he said, "Fear not them which kill the body, but are not able to kill the soul" (Matt. 10:28). In short, if you examine the Scriptures, you will find that the inspired writers uniformly keep up this distinction on which I am insisting. Their faith was that death was not an annihilation of existence but only a change in the mode of it. It is of the highest importance that you believe this doctrine, for without it you lose the influence of all those motives which give vigor and worth to human actions.

If you admit the idea that your existence will terminate

with the present life, your love of virtue will diminish and die. If there is nothing beyond this life, you will succumb to your impulses and feelings since eternal consequences of our actions may be entirely disregarded.

If you regard your own interest or that of society, never depart from the doctrine of the soul's immortality. The consequences of a belief in the opposite doctrine are so manifestly dangerous and evil that you may rest assured it cannot be founded on truth.

Remember not only that you are immortal but also that you are accountable. It is impossible for God to form a rational being and not bind that being under moral law so long as he shall exist. This law flows from the absolute perfection and supremacy of the divine nature. When we say that God infinitely loves us, it naturally follows that he is to be infinitely loved by us. Moral obligation therefore arises from the nature of God and, like that, is unchangeable and eternal—that is it comes to man from God. Morality is not the invention of the hearts of men.

At death your soul remains. Do not imagine this change in your state will exempt you from a responsibility for your conduct.

A sense of your eternal accountability will lift you above the groveling pursuits of vice and furnish a perpetual excitement in the cultivation of those virtues which alone can render you worthy and happy. Nothing can be more absurd, nothing more dangerous in its consequences, than the assertion that men are not subject to trial in the courts of God. If man is at liberty to conduct his life as he pleases without a liability of being called into account, he will no longer care about either his character or his actions.

Let me urge upon you the importance of the preceding beliefs concerning the existence of God, the immortality of the soul, and future responsibility. The world is more indebted to these three doctrines for its order and government than to all other causes. These doctrines as to their full extent and influence are only known by the revelation of the Word. If you discard them, you sap the energy from every virtuous ideal; you undermine the foundations of society and level the human to that of the brute.

You are now entering on a vast, dangerous, and tumultuous theater. A scene opens before you that will demand all your abilities and talents in support of religion and liberty.

I now give you, gentlemen, my parting benediction, wishing you may live honored, respected, and beloved in this world; and in the next shine like stars in the firmament forever.

On Religion and Government

Otis Thompson

13

Introduction

As we have seen, Rhode Island College provided a steady voice advocating religious liberty for all. Does this mean these advocates wanted to separate God from government or from public life?

Otis Thompson's 1798 address makes clear that a religious people and leaders who share these basic convictions are essential for a nation that loves liberty and justice.

Background

During the Revolutionary War the campus of Rhode Island College (modern-day Brown University) was commandeered by the British for use as barracks and later used by the French as a hospital for soldiers. From 1776 to 1782 the buildings saw rough service, and after the war the college board asked the new Congress of the United States to cough up 1309 pounds, 3 shillings, and 2 pence to aid with repairs. Congress did indeed provide financial assistance . . . ten years later (in the form of $2,779.13, less than a third of what the college requested). During Otis Thompson's education the college was still operating as best it could in spite of its damaged structures. The college board brainstormed ways to lend prestige to the rather dilapidated appearance of commencement ceremonies and finally hit upon graduation robes and hats. Alumni were required to wear them although the flowing robes made for uncomfortably hot attire.

In one of these ceremonies, Otis Thompson took the stage to deliver his "Oration Urging the Necessity of Religion as the Only Permanent Basis of Civil Government." Thompson's audience was probably growing restless—there had been twelve presentations before his that morning, including: "A Poem on Faction"; "A Dissertation on the Evils of Luxury"; "A Dispute on the Question: Which Is More Conducive to Virtue, Prosperity or Adversity?"; two Latin addresses, and an "Intermediate Oration on the Immortality of Brutes."

Thompson's was the thirteenth of fourteen speeches, but fortunately the almost twenty-two-year-old had chosen a topic that was foremost on everyone's minds: the French Revolution's reign of terror. "Turn your eyes toward the bloody fields of France, and view the reality," Thompson urged. "See there the genuine product of atheism: virtue driven into exile; the laws of God and the rights of human nature insulted and trampled upon." He had captured the attention of the audience.

It is not surprising that Thompson chose to close his college career with a speech on religion. He actively studied theology and spent two years as a tutor at Rhode Island College partly in order to fill the duties of librarian and so have access to the library's theological works. The young man from Massachusetts would become Reverend Thompson by age twenty-four and spend over twenty-five years pastoring a church in Rehoboth, Massachusetts.

Thompson is remembered as an "acute metaphysical thinker," a man with an imperious will who held to his opinions and would brook no opposition. He was a scholarly man, publishing numerous sermons and funeral orations, editing the *Hopkinsian Magazine*, and supervising the theological studies of fifteen students. Among his students were Moses and Tyler Thatcher, the grandsons of Rev. Peter Thatcher who was the first pastor of the Second Congregational Church, as well as Jason Chamberlain, a bright lad who went on to become a professor at Vermont University.

Speech

Otis Thompson
Rhode Island College
September, 1798

An Oration Urging the Necessity of Religion as the Only Permanent Basis of Civil Government at the Commencement of Rhode Island College

If you discard the doctrines of the existence of God, the immortality of the soul, and the future responsibility, you enervate every virtuous sentiment, you undermine the foundations of society, and level the human to the brute creation.

—President Maxcy's Address, September 5, 1798

Human nature is ever prone to extremes. The preceding was an age of intolerance and bigotry. The present is an age of licentiousness and infidelity.

Certain modern politicians therefore, who became enthusiastic in the cause of liberty and were roused to indignation at the horrors of persecution, have proceeded to banish all religious considerations from their political creed. Even more they pronounce religion itself an imposition on mankind, a mere artifice invented by despots to terrify their subjects into quivering submission.

The truth is that the security of government requires two

essential attributes. First, legislators must be men of virtue. Second, a secure nation requires that among the people there must be a widespread view that embraces both virtue and religious obligation. It is not enough to believe that we must do that which is good; we must believe that this is also the desire of Almighty God.

The principles of freedom require that the government should never dictate our faith, yet freedom will not survive if the hearts of our people fail to adhere to God and his standards of virtue.

Even if our laws are both good and just, they will not be practiced any further than is consistent with the common wishes of the public. Some more powerful agent must guide the current of water in its proper channels and direct it where to flow. A legislature could as easily attempt to stop the rising tides of the ocean as to attempt to impose a law which is contrary to widely held views in public opinion. Therefore, it is indispensable that the public mind be formed on the principles and guided by the precepts of morality and the Christian religion!

Let us now for a moment reverse the picture. Let us imagine to ourselves a people who deride the idea of God, who disbelieve that they will face an eternal future of rewards and punishments and treat the solemn commands of God with contempt. Such thinking produces conflicts between rulers and the people inflamed with mutual distrust and jealously which perpetually feed the flame of faction and discord. In such a world the object of government is unlimited domination of the people and the annihilation of all justice.

What is the consequence when all religious principles are abolished? Turn your eyes toward the bloody fields of France and view the reality. See there the genuine product of atheism: virtue driven into exile; the laws of God and the rights of human nature insulted and trampled upon.

Our liberties are in jeopardy. Let us with godly eloquence arise to oppose the torrent of licentiousness. Thus shall the virtues of our pious ancestors ever inspire the hearts of Americans and our nation be rescued from impending ruin. Thus shall our Constitution, unmoved by the convulsions of empire, survive the depredations of ages, and stand as monumental testimony in support of this great truth, that a government whose pillars are virtue and religion can never dissolve but with the dissolution of the universe.

In Defense
of the Bible
Asa Messer

14

Introduction

The cultivation of knowledge and reason is viewed by some as not only the activity of higher education but also as the foundation of all truth. Asa Messer, the third president of Rhode Island College, explained a better way to the students of 1799.

Messer argued for the centrality of the Bible to all knowledge, truth, and life itself. It is an eloquent and convincing defense of the supremacy of God's Word.

Background

Asa Messer was ten years older than Jonathan Maxcy when he was appointed as the third president of Brown University

(Rhode Island College), but he found that Maxcy had left large shoes to fill. Messer had graduated from Brown in 1790 under President Manning and during his formative years had felt a strong call to pursue religious studies. As a young man Messer said he experienced a renewal of personal faith in Jesus Christ partly through the influence of Jonathan Maxcy. Maxcy actually baptized Messer and helped Messer gain a license to preach at First Baptist Church in Providence. However, even after receiving his ordination, Messer remained at Brown tutoring students in Greek, Latin, and Hebrew. In 1796 Messer was instated as the professor of learned languages and three years later was promoted to Brown's professor of mathematics and natural philosophy. By this point Messer had been living at Brown for over ten years so he was the logical candidate to replace Maxcy.

One of Messer's friends, the Reverend Edwards Amasa Park, penned the following description of the active American scholar:

> No one who has ever seen him can ever forget him. His individuality was made unmistakable by his physical frame. This, while it was above the average height, was also in breadth an emblem of the expansiveness of his mental capacity. A "long head" was vulgarly ascribed to him, but it was breadth that marked his forehead; there was an expressive breadth

in his maxillary bones; his broad shoulders were a sign of the weight which he was able to bear; his manner of walking was a noticeable symbol of the reach of his mind; he swung his cane far and wide as he walked, and no observer would doubt that he was an independent man; he gesticulated broadly as he preached; his enunciation was forcible, and now and then overwhelming, sometimes shrill, but was characterized by a breadth of tone and a prolonged emphasis which added to its momentum, and made an indelible impress on the memory. His pupils, when they had been unfaithful, trembled before his expansive frown, as it portended a rebuke which would well-nigh devour them; and they felt a dilating of the whole soul, when they were greeted with his good and honest and broad smile.

Speech

Asa Messer
Rhode Island College
Sunday (Prior to Commencement), 1799

A Discourse to the Senior Class

It is not my design, nor indeed is it possible on this occasion to bring forward all the arguments in favor of the Bible. Let it now be sufficient to observe that on the basis a man rejects the Bible, he must reject the authenticity of all ancient records. He must deny that there were ever such men as Homer, Virgil, Cicero, Alexander, Caesar, or Charles V. He must deny that a revelation from God can possibly be established by sufficient evidence. He must assert that all the doctrines of the Bible are the inventions of men though they transcend human inventions as much as the sun transcends a candle. He must assert that the authors of the Bible were vile, conniving impostors though they have every mark of uprightness, truthfulness, and kindness. He must assert that the whole Christian world and, among the rest, that Boyle, Newton, Locke, Clarke, Addison, Barrows, and numerous others, though the most splendid monuments of human genius and learning, were nothing more than a horde of ignorant, bigoted dupes. And he must give up all assurance that he has any soul more than a beast or that he shall ever survive the slumbers of death.

Hence it is essential to a sound mind to give full credit to the whole contents of the Bible. There can be nothing more absurd than to believe that the Bible is the word of God and yet to believe that it contains anything unreasonable, contradictory, or unimportant. Whatsoever God reveals must certainly coincide with the nature of God, and hence can never interfere with right reason. When our reason is once satisfied that God has given us a revelation, and what are its contents then, however much those contents may differ from our reason, still our reason itself must acknowledge they are reasonable, for nothing unreasonable can proceed from God. Accordingly, all the doctrines however difficult or challenging which are contained in the Bible are justly entitled to our full belief.

We can conclude that it is as great a sign of folly to deny the existence of God as it is to deny the most plain and certain proposition in Euclid and his teachings on geometry. None but a fool, none but a madman, can say in his heart, "There is no God." In large, indelible letters which radiate with goodness, God has written his existence and perfections on your heart and your soul as well as on every object that you can perceive with your senses. I exhort you, open your eyes and read what you see: nature itself proclaims the existence of God. If you will not believe, you must give up all pretensions to soundness of mind, and you may well lament that you have spent so much time and labor and money in this institution. Yes, if you will not believe there is a God, you must adopt the ghastly, murderous doctrine that you have no Creator, no Preserver, no Benefactor; that you sprang you know not from what; that you are bound you know not where; that there is no virtue, no vice, no heaven, no hell, no immortal state, no day of righteous retribution, no nothing which can elevate you above an ox.

O cruel, foolish, desperate doctrine!

We can also conclude that nothing but extreme folly or wickedness can induce a man to desire the destruction of the Bible. A belief in the Bible is perfectly suited to exalt the dignity and value of man and to make him a better citizen, a better neighbor, a better father, husband, son. The mind of man cannot even imagine a system of morals than the system contained in the Bible. Hence he who desires the destruction of the Bible not only opposes all the forcible evidences in its favor but also desires the destruction of the most effective antidote ever administered for the sickness and sorrows of man. Let me exhort you, young men, to exterminate unbelief forever from your hearts. Indulge not even a wish that the Bible may be false for our faith is very apt to follow our wishes.

As you glory in that natural reason which elevates you above the beasts and that improved reason which elevates you above most of your fellowmen, let me exhort you to read the Bible and to examine its evidences with that candid spirit which is ever essential to the investigation of truth. Let your minds be wholly unbiased by prejudice or passion and willing to embrace truth from any direction. If this were my last, dying speech, I would exhort you to believe and to revere the Bible; to treasure its precious information in your minds and hearts and to make that the regulator of your thoughts, words, and actions. Remember that there is now no other name than the name of Jesus given under heaven among men whereby you must be saved and that he is able and willing to save them to the uttermost who come to God through him. I beseech you to go to God in his name and to accept the overtures of peace and pardon proclaimed in the gospel.

A Faithful Guide

Jedidiah Morse

15

Introduction

Higher education proceeds upon the theory of "open inquiry"—at least in theory. An increasing proportion of the institutions of higher education are so one-sided in their liberal and secularist presuppositions that any claim they are considering all sides of a question must be seriously questioned.

How then should a Christian student approach higher education? Should we read only those things that confirm our convictions? Or should we also read things that have played an important role in human society whether for good or evil?

Jedidiah Morse gives the graduates of Philips Academy sound advice as they were about to head off to the various colleges of their day. Find a reliable guide, he says. An experienced believer who can help the student navigate the waters of inquiry is essential.

A faithful professor at a faithful Christian college is the best source for such a guide today. However, keep in mind the words of J. Vernon McGee, who said that there are "believers, nonbelievers, and make-believers." We can find too many colleges which used to be composed of believers that are now dominated by make-believers.

Choose your guide wisely.

Background

July 9, 1799—When Jedidiah Morse addressed the young students of Phillips Academy in his gentle manner and smooth voice, expressing his hope that "hundreds of amiable, ingenious, and pious youths, educated on this foundation, and dispersed through our country will be so many public blessings," he was deeply concerned about such turbulent events as the French Revolution and the political and religious changes the newly fledged United States itself was undergoing. He wanted the students at Phillips Academy, who had their sights set on Yale, Harvard, Princeton, Dartmouth, and other prestigious centers of learning to grasp the notion of responsibility. Morse believed that men who were privileged with the leisure and opportunity to pursue higher education were under great obligation to their country, God, and posterity.

His own son Samuel F. B. Morse attended the Academy, and Morse urged him to spend his time wisely. Morse Sr. actually wrote out a daily routine for Samuel to follow, the goal of which was to fashion a reverent Christian gentleman out of a headstrong lad. Morse wanted his son to be thrifty, humble, well mannered, and yet inspired to strive for personal distinction. "Take care to read your rules everyday and observe them strictly," Morse wrote to Samuel:

1. Rise early in the morning—read a chapter in the Bible, and say your prayers. Read the Bible in course. The Old Testament in the morning. The New Testament at night. . . .

2. After a serious performance of these religious duties, comb your head and wash your face, hands and mouth in cold water, not hastily and slightly but thoroughly. . . .

3. Get your morning lesson well—behave decently at breakfast. Go regularly and seasonably to the Academy. While there, in study hours, attend to your lesson, and get it thoroughly, and try to be the best scholar in your class.

4. In play hours, while at play, behave manly and honorably. Avoid everything low, mean, indecent, or unfair. And endeavour to play in such a manner as that all may wish to have you on their side.

Morse was not asking anything from his son that he himself had not personally experienced. During his divinity studies at Yale (1786), he held himself on a rigorous schedule. For thirty years he was head pastor of a congregation in Charlestown, Massachusetts. He was engaged in the debates surrounding Unitarianism, Deism, atheism, and Calvinism and three times a week addressed his flock from the pulpit of his Congregational church (which stood in the shadow of Bunker Hill). Generally, his sermons would last for well over two hours, and one historian estimated that a faithful member of Morse's church would have heard over seven thousand sermons in the course of a lifetime.

On top of his ministry, Morse managed to correspond with prominent men such as John Adams, the bishop of London, and the French foreign minister Talleyrand, Noah Webster, Benjamin Silliman, and Jeremy Belknap. Many of these men he met through his infatuation with American geography. Certainly Morse was more famous as a geographer than a minister. By 1800 Morse's books about the American landscape were second in popularity only to Webster's dictionary and the Holy Bible, and most homes had a well-thumbed copy of his *American Geography* (1789) on the shelf. New editions of his child-friendly textbooks as well as weightier compilations earned Morse the informal title "Father of American Geography." His *Universal Geography of the United States* is still cited today. Ralph Brown notes that Morse's contributions to geography are a literary declaration of independence from the Old World; no longer could the United States be seen through European eyes.

Morse enjoyed friendship with many notable Americans. He dined in Philadelphia with Benjamin Franklin and at Mount Vernon with George Washington, a man for whom Morse held the deepest respect both politically and personally. In fact, Morse was an outspoken Federalist; and his support of Washington, Adams, Jay, and Hamilton got him into some trouble in August 1795. Morse was confronted by a mob angry about the Jay treaty (they were burning Mr. Jay in effigy), and he jumped at the chance to defend his friend. Unfortunately, an angry protester leapt at Morse with a brickbat and struck him on the head, an incident which Morse dealt with in characteristic good humor. In fact, shortly afterward when an anxious friend called to inquire on the severity Morse's injury, whether it had harmed his brain, Morse replied, "Certainly not. No, if I had had any brains, I should not have been there."

Morse's patriotism did not go unnoticed. In 1799, General Washington read Dr. Morse's discourse on the United State's controversy with France; and in a letter dated February 28, Washington praises Morse for his political activism and factual arguments. Apparently Washington had read both Morse's "Fast Day" sermon of May 9, 1798 and his "Thanksgiving" sermon of November 29, 1798, in which Morse expressed a Federalist's alarm at French interference in American affairs.

Although he approved of Washington's judgment in

most areas, Jedidiah Morse was strongly opposed to Thomas Jefferson's presence at the helm of the nation. Morse felt that a man unaccustomed to attending public worship (an unashamed and professed infidel) was unfit to direct a country that stood on the bedrock of Christian tradition. "Unhappy indeed must that Christian people be," Morse warned, "whose Chief Magistrate is an Atheist." Morse felt grateful that George Washington had died before Jefferson acceded to ruler in chief but lamented that "ever since his death the clouds seem to have been gathering for a storm."

For Morse the storm began raging in the 1800s after Harvard appointed a Unitarian professor, and he wrote that the United States was "most imminently threatened with a revolution which will deeply and lastingly affect the cause of evangelical truth." He warned Harvard that by abandoning its theological moorings it was steering a course of destruction. "[T]his ancient fountain will be poisoned, and its streams henceforth are the bane of evangelical religion."[6]

Speech

Jedediah Morse
Phillips Academy
July 9, 1799

An Address to the Students
at Phillips Academy in Andover

Young Gentlemen,

It is with emotions of heartfelt satisfaction that I rise, on behalf of the trustees of this institution, to address you.

You have an opportunity put into your hands to obtain wisdom above most of the youth of your age and standing. May God give you hearts to be faithful as you pursue your tasks. Follow the path of duty, honor, and happiness. You are now laying a foundation on which to erect a superstructure for both worlds. The characters and habits you are now forming, the direction you now take will be likely to continue through this life and to determine your future eternal condition.

To you, young gentlemen of the senior class who are about to take leave of this seminary and enter the university, permit us to observe that the transition you are about to make will form an important era in your lives. In the present disorganized state of society in general, your temptations will be numerous, your dangers great. You will have need, therefore, to be strongly fortified against the infidel and insidious philosophy which has produced such extensive havoc and desolation in the principles and morals of mankind. While we would encourage free inquiry as the only way to arrive at the knowledge of truth, we would by all means and especially in this seductive and demoralizing age recommend that your early inquiries be pursued under the direction of an experienced and skilled guide.

Your youthful curiosity . . . would often lead you upon enchanted ground where you will easily be bewildered and lost. It would prompt you to read those books that have been poured into our country by thousands and circulated with much art and industry among young people and which are replete with concealed but deadly poison to your principles and morals. Concerned as we feel for your welfare, we would affectionately urge you individually to solicit some faithful, well-principled, and experienced friend to prescribe for you your course of reading. By doing this and adhering to the advice you may receive, you will not only avoid ensnaring and corrupting books which might ruin you for both worlds, but you would also prevent a great waste of time; acquire more and more useful knowledge, and avail yourselves of others' experience.

Cultivate a kind, benevolent, friendly, and peaceful disposition. And let these traits guide you in gentleness and sweetness of manners. Be open, honest, yet discreet in all your behavior and never deceive or disappoint those who have placed confidence in you. Avoid pride, haughtiness, and scorn.

Meek, modest, and obedient behavior will exalt you in the view of every person deserving your esteem. Form and cherish early habits of industry and attention to business. Be orderly and methodical in your amusements and literary pursuits, and be regular and punctual in the performance of your social, civil, and religious duties. Avoid idleness and idlers as the destroyer of your happiness and your reputation. Despise everything which is vulgar, disgraceful, and selfish. Abhor everything that is profane, scandalous, obscene, or immodest. Religiously preserve purity in your morals, conversation, and a becoming dignity and manliness in your whole way of life, generously seeking to promote public and private good.

Above all, young gentlemen, and as that which alone gives a value and adds luster and beauty to every other qualification, see first of all and seek earnestly and as the chief good, what is justly and emphatically styled, the one thing needful, the pearl of great price, and never give up the pursuit till you obtain it. Salvation is the treasure of ultimate value; without it, though you should be loaded with all the wealth and honor this world can yield, you will be poor indeed. Never believe a person can deserve your friendship or be your friend who despises it either on principle or practice. A person of this character may be your companion, your flatterer, your seducer, but believe me young gentlemen, he can never be your friend. You assuredly can have no good reason to expect that he will be faithful to you who is not so faithful to his conscience and his God.

Finally, my young friends, *true* religion will ennoble and beautify your minds, sanctify and regulate your beliefs, purify and comfort your hearts, and qualify you to be ready and extensively useful to your fellow creatures by your example and conversation; and what is more than all the rest, it will make you wise to eternal life.

Truth versus Reason

Ebenezer Fitch

16

Introduction

Many today equate the principles of the French Revolution (1789–1799) with those of the American Revolution. Upon this pretext some scholars base their argument that the secular enlightenment was the source of American liberty. However, most Americans alive during the period would have rejected this argument.

Why? Because they understood that knowledge elevated, worshipped, and separated from the knowledge of God becomes a destructive, violent force that never results in peace or liberty.

It is incredibly important for today's students in America to understand the distinction between the French and American

Revolutions—not merely for historical purposes but for the purpose of learning to distinguish between true knowledge, which always starts with God, and its humanistic counterfeit.

Background

In 1777, Ebenezer Fitch matriculated at Yale and was the valedictorian of his class, no small feat in light of the political and economic turbulence facing the colonies. Despite many obstacles Fitch and his classmates managed to complete their studies. According to the biographer of Timothy Dwight, the spring of 1777 saw "the college broken up." For the past several years tempers had been high at Yale. In 1765 Yale's administration had to restrain Whig students from engaging in a potentially ugly street fight with Tory locals. Tempers kept rising so the students "left New Haven to pursue their studies during the summer under their respective tutors, in places less exposed to the sudden incursions of the enemy."

Fitch's senior class spent the summer in Wethersfield under the supervision of then tutor Dr. Timothy Dwight. Political unrest and patriotism were fomenting in the streets, and every day brought new tensions between Loyalists and Rebels. British troops were quartered in the city, and by spring things had reached a stage where an open commencement ceremony on Yale grounds was deemed impossible. This was a disappointment to Fitch, whose journal records his memory of the commencement day of 1776:

July 24, 1776, Commencement day. It was a private one. C. Goodrich delivered the Cliosophic oration—an excellent one and handsomely delivered. Strong and Lyman gave a forensic dispute on the question *Whether all religions ought to be tolerated.* The subject was well and ably discussed. Porter, Howe, and Mitchel spoke a dialogue, and Russell pronounced the Valedictory oration: all well performed. But to crown all, Mr. Dwight delivered an excellent oration on the present state and future growth and importance of this country. It was written and delivered in a masterly manner. My collegiate life is fast drawing to a close. One year more and I shall have done. The time is too short; I wish it were longer.

For Yale's graduation of 1777, the senior class returned to New Haven to receive their diplomas. The leadership of the college for a few brief moments ignored the rumors of war and congratulated these newest initiates into the small pool of homegrown colonial academics.

It was a formative period in Fitch's life. He was convinced that God had spared his life from sickness, war, and woe and in return he was "under great obligations to devote (himself) wholly to the service of Him." Personal piety eventually led Fitch to receive the presidency of Williams College. Before that position Fitch tutored at Yale from 1780 to 1783. He also tried and failed to start his own business, eventually concluding that he was destined to be an educator, not a businessman. In 1790, Fitch became the preceptor of a free academy for boys in Williamstown, Massachusetts. Fitch taught mental science, laws of nations, and classes on moral philosophy. He also required his students to be familiar with the Westminster Catechism, and he often preached Sunday sermons to reinforce sound theology. Within two years Fitch had raised the academic standards to such a degree that the Williamstown Free School was able to petition the state legislature for the status of Williams College.

Speech

Ebenezer Fitch
Williams College
September 1, 1799

Useful Knowledge and Religion, Recommended to the Pursuit and Improvement of the Young; in a Discourse, Addressed to the Candidates for the Baccalaureate in Williams College

Covet earnestly the best gifts: and yet shew I unto you a more excellent way.

—1 Corinthians 12:31

Man, the last and most noble piece of divine workman-ship in this world, claims the greatest share of God's attention. Man is distinguished in several respects from the lower orders of God's creation. In the kingdom of animals, their powers are limited and may be enlarged or improved but a little whereas the potential of man's capacity to improve is nearly unlimited. The capacity of the beast for enjoyment is scanty and consists of only the low, gross pleasures of sense. Man may learn to enjoy the pleasures that rise to greatness— those that are fitted for the noblest intellectual and moral pleasures.

It is therefore self-evident that man is greatly distinguished from the inferior orders of creatures. Is it not strange then that man's boastful philosophy has concluded that man's eternal destiny is no different from that of the beast: to perish forever and be forgotten? Reason and revelation concur in their decision that man has a far higher and nobler destiny. The breath of the Almighty has made him immortal and given him powers capable of nearly endless progressive improvement in knowledge and virtue.

But the mental powers and faculties of man were not made to grow like vegetables or animal bodies, without any labor or exertion of his own. They need diligent culture, vigorous exercise, the aids of science, and the beneficial influence of religion to bring them to maturity. The cultivation of the heart should keep pace with the growth and enlargement of the mental powers. Intellectual endowments, natural or acquired, can never alone raise man to the elevated rank in the scale of being which his Maker designed him to hold. Virtue and religion unite to make us truly happy and noble. We are thereby raised to the true dignity of a rational immortal creature. "Covet earnestly," says the apostle, "the best gifts: and yet shew I unto you a more excellent way" (1 Cor. 12:31).

Natural gifts, talents, and powers are such as God their Author has been pleased to make them. Thus one man has a gift or talent which enables him to excel in one walk of science or profession, and another in another. "A man is born, not made," said the Romans; and the same observation is equally applicable to every natural gift or talent. There are also supernatural gifts of miracles, of prophesying, of healing the sick, and of speaking or interpreting an unknown language; . . . but it is the acquired gifts or talents that I mean principally to treat and which I would recommend as objects worthy of your diligent and strenuous pursuit.

Oratory, or the skillful use of language, is valuable principally as the mean of social interaction. The man who becomes proficient in this skill acquires a commanding influence over the opinions, passions, and actions of his fellowmen. He has it in his power not merely to please, instruct, and persuade but also to convince, arouse, animate, and impel. Paul of Tarsus was celebrated, even by the learned heathen of that day as one of the first orators of the age. And to what a noble purpose was his oratory applied! Thousands now in heaven converted under his preaching can testify and will testify forever.

Need I undertake to point out to you, young gentlemen, the numerous advantages and uses of oratory? Is it not one of the first qualifications, one of the most brilliant ornaments of the lawyer and the statesman as well as of the minister of God? Diligently cultivate this talent; earnestly covet this highly valuable and useful gift.

General science is a talent or gift of extensive application and utility. What a debt of gratitude is due to men of such eminent erudition as Bacon, and Boyle, and Newton, and Locke!

But to become well known for general knowledge, great abilities, much study, and extraordinary diligence are required. Few, therefore, shine as general scholars while many become well regarded for some specific department of science. Seek to learn as your greatest priority those branches of knowledge that are the most useful to your fellowman. The mere scholar, the man of idle speculation, who pursues his research solely for the purpose of gratifying his own tastes or curiosity or simply desires fame, is a useless drone in society. It should always be your aim to improve your knowledge for some valuable purpose.

In every society laws are necessary to regulate the civil conduct of individuals. A thorough knowledge of these laws has become a challenging and important study. To understand them in their true spirit and principle, explain them clearly, and apply them with precision and justice constitutes the business of a useful and necessary profession. If to your fund of general knowledge you add the hard-earned treasures of judicial science, you will have a gift which, if used with honor and integrity, will procure you wealth and reputation and be of essential service to your fellowmen.

Useful knowledge is a gift of high importance to the minister of Christ. In no other business or calling is it so necessary that a man should be a scholar as well as a Christian. God has been, if I may so say, at infinite trouble and expense to rescue us from misery and procure us happiness in the coming world. We are redeemed not by corruptible things as silver and gold but by the precious blood of the Son of God. Had all the angels of heaven died for us, it would have availed nothing. Divine justice demanded an infinite ransom. The death of the great Emmanuel alone could be accepted as an adequate atonement for the guilt of fallen man. Such was the evil of sin, and such the worth of the soul in the view of omniscience! Through Christ's atoning blood, pardon, peace, and eternal life are offered to guilty men. Thus the ministers of the Prince of peace need all the aids of human learning as well as the teachings of his Spirit to qualify them for their important trust. They must be able by sound doctrine to stop the mouths of naysayers.

Shall the man rich in knowledge hoard his treasure as a miser does his gold? Shameful selfishness! Forbid it honor, patriotism, piety! Talents for usefulness should not be buried in a napkin. To whom much is given, of them much is required both by God and their country. Men of abilities, science, and virtue easily acquire influence. They can do much for the encouragement of learning, true patriotism, and good morals.

In this day especially, when every civil and religious institution is threatened with ruin; when a spirit of vandalism, hostile to rational liberty and to everything dear to us as men and Christians has already devastated the fairest parts of Europe, every man of science, every friend to virtue and his country is called upon to exert every effort to stop the raging torrent. You cannot be innocent if you remain an idle bystander while the enemies of truth seek to eradicate good government, morality, and religion from the earth.

Stand then at your posts and die like men rather than allow that liberty for which our fathers bled (together with that government which they established with so much wisdom, and that religion which they held dearer than life) to be sacrificed at the unhallowed shrine of atheism and French philosophy.

Even while you abhor these dangerous falsehoods, take pity upon those that are its victims even if they are willing victims.

Before they passed into eternity, philosophers like Hume and Voltaire attacked God's truth, promoted infidelity and vice with clever wit and sophistication. But how valuable are those talents to them today? Their talents are now little more than flaming torches to light them to the lowest pit of their infernal prison and show them in tenfold horrors the regions of eternal darkness. What would they now give for one cheering ray of that heavenly religion which they hooted and despised? How they now long for one drop of his atoning blood whom with the rage and malice of fiends they so often reviled and blasphemed?

God claims your best services. They are justly and unchangeably his to command. Think often on what you owe to yourselves, to your friends, to your country and your God. Labor more to be virtuous than to be learned—to be good than to be great. Value less the applause of men than the testimony of a good conscience and the approval of your Maker. The period allotted you for active usefulness is short, but the consequences of improving or neglecting it will run through eternity.

We commend you to the grace, protection, and blessing of Almighty God. May he . . . crown your faithful and benevolent services here with immortal glory and happiness in the world above!

A Time to Fight

Tristam Burges

17

Introduction

In the last fifty years, American colleges have often been the locus of antiwar protests. "War is not the answer" scream the banners and placards.

Young America looked at the world differently. War is never desirable, but sometimes it is necessary. The use of war for aggression or conquest is utterly incompatible with the American spirit. But, as we see in the words of Tristam Burges, when it is necessary to defend justice and liberty, men of courage stand up and fight.

Background

Commencement speakers often have a difficult time mounting 'the podium, and twenty-six-year-old Tristam Burges had more reason than most to be nervous. Burges had been assigned to give the valedictory address to Rhode Island College's graduating class of 1796, despite the fact that his first attempt at public speaking had been a fiasco. The man who was destined to be one of America's greatest lawyers and whose eloquence his biographer would describe as "supreme over judges, jurors, and spectators," had to mount the chapel stage and face his fears.

Four short years before, while enrolled in a small Massachusetts school, Burges had tried to overcome his slight speech impediment. He had stood up before his classmates to deliver a speech but found himself tongue-tied. After a series of unintelligible syllables, Burges stepped from the spotlight in confusion and great embarrassment. Afterwards, one of his comrades mocked him suggesting that he "get someone to do his speaking for him."[7] The comment galled Burges. He resolved to master his mouth and marched out into a nearby clearing to practice speaking. "Day by day, amid the cool shades of the neighboring forest, he labored to change his stammering utterances to distinct articulations."[8] His labor paid off. Friends in the audience on the morning of September 7, 1796 were impressed; and Henry Bowen, his biographer, wrote, "When on stage for Commencement, he appeared to so much advantage, his friends were grateful that he had surmounted numerous obstacles."[9]

In conquering weaknesses Burges was merely acting according to the pattern of self-discipline he had followed since his earliest youth. Born in 1771 in Plymouth County, Massachusetts, to active yeoman-patriot John Burges, Tristam Burges did not have access to much formal education. An older sister taught him to read while his father passed on what arithmetic he knew from his cooper's trade, and an ex-sea captain neighbor gave him lessons and books on navigation. That, combined with twelve weeks of formal schooling late in his teen years, was all the formal education Burges received until he was twenty-one. However, "he had read every book that he could buy, beg, or borrow," including medical dictionaries and Latin and Greek classics.[10]

During his college days Burges attended class and lectures for six hours and then spent another six hours studying law. He "devoted day and night to Law," and when he was admitted to the bar in Rhode Island in 1799 at the age of twenty-nine, he was "thoroughly versed in all the principles of that profound science."[11]

In 1799, Burges was a second time asked to speak at the Rhode Island commencement ceremonies, and he unleashed with fiery eloquence his disapproval of the French Revolution, urging his audience to ready America for peace or war.

In his audience sat fifteen-year-old John Pitman, who would go on to be appointed by President James Monroe as

Judge of the U.S. District Court for the District of Rhode Island, and serve in that office for forty years; Nathan Fellows Dixon, future Rhode Island Senator, future father of a Rhode Island Senator, and future grandfather of a Rhode Island Senator; Jeremiah Chaplin, future president of the college; Franklin Greene, future cotton tycoon; future Reverend Alvin Toby; and dozens more remarkable American businessmen, lawyers, preachers, and educators.

Burges lived amid the tumult that characterized the city of Providence. It was a hotbed of patriotism and industrialization—a strange jumble of slave traders, intellectuals, soldiers, lawyers, farmers, and doctors. Its ports were home base to men who ran privateer ships up and down the East Coast,[12] as well as to molasses merchants who dabbled in the triangle trade of rum for slaves for molasses for rum.[13]

Burges was active in the academic community as well as in the political arena. He served as a representative to Rhode Island's General Assembly (1811) and was elected Chief Justice of the Supreme Court of Rhode Island (1817). Burges opposed the policies and person of Andrew Jackson, instead allying himself with John Quincy Adams, which gained him a seat in the U.S. House of Representatives (1825). Burges was also named professor of oratory and belles letters at Brown (1815), and his was an audible voice in the academic community until his death at Watchemoket on October 13, 1853. His biographer Henry Bowden writes that "when he spoke, the

Court House was often thronged, and none listened without a tribute of admiration."

Speech

Tristam Burges
Rhode Island College
September 4, 1799

War, Necessary, Just and Beneficial:
An Oration Pronounced on Commencement
at Rhode Island College

Be ready for Thine adversary.

—Shakespeare, A Mother to Her Son

This festive anniversary, this civic and classical parade, and even the shining countenances of this numerous assembly give strong testimony to the general happiness that prevails in our country. But there are signs that we can also see which clearly indicate that our situation of delightful peace may be shattered by violence.

When we behold that foreign flag, unfolding its red bosom to the winds of heaven, we feel the possibility of war. The history of the world is but a story of war. War has become an art. And while war may be inevitable, at times it is also necessary. If we are categorically unwilling to wage war, then we are also unable to resist injury. Only a brave resistance of those who would do us harm, with the willingness to go to war if necessary to prove our resolve is the only remaining restraint on the evil desires of the wicked. Resistance is the only hill that rises in opposition to an ocean of oppression. If that hill is removed, the waves of oppression will of a certainty rush in and deluge the moral world.

If resistance is unjust, why do we sympathize with the injured, or why do we feel the same resentment at those who do us wrong? God Almighty gave us just resentment of evil. It is the imprint of God on our spirit which swells our hearts with indignation, sparkles in our eye, nerves our arm against the wretch who dares abuse the freedom bestowed upon us by our common Creator. If a war of defense is unjust, why have we a principle of self-preservation? Why do we have our country, our friends, our own being, if we are forbidden to raise our arm in their defense?

The doctrine of nonresistance goes to the utter destruction of all virtue. If we may not defend our friends, our country, our brother-men, then friendship, and patriotism, and philanthropy, and benevolence are vices. Jesus said, he who takes the weapons of *aggression* shall perish by them, but let him who has no sword of *defense* sell his coat and buy one.

The intention of a just war is preservation. Though millions have fallen in battle, though thousands of hills have been soaked with blood, and though the flame of many a city under siege has cast a crimson edge on the dark bosom of midnight—all revealing the terrible price of war, yet we must observe that often nations are preserved by war alone. War has once been the salvation of our country. It wrested us not from the parental embrace of a mother state but from the iron arms of tyranny. It gave us independence and prepared us for the first nutrition by which we have grown to our present national maturity.

War has given the world its most illustrious characters. It furnished Homer with a theme for deathless voice and opened to Achilles a field for immortal achievements. Had war never been, Washington had never been and the world had forever lost the model and the admiration of all succeeding time.

War gives men the indescribable delight of defending all that is dear to them. There are those who, to redeem others from danger, would willingly die with a sense of deep honor. I, this moment, behold men here today who have marched barefoot many a winter night and amid the storm of many a battle, wished no greater joy than to throw their naked bosoms between their country and her foes. What must they have felt when they saw their country safe?

If war be inevitable, if nations will violate our rights, if a war of defense be justified by our own feelings, the eternal principles of self-preservation, the example of heaven, and the awful mandates of him who has all power in all worlds; if wars save nations, demolish despotism, throw open the doors of timeless honor, and bestow the unequaled delight of defending all that can endear the possession of life; if war does all these things, let us banish all reluctance and all timidity at the approach of battle.

If at any time in any region of the earth, any nation might apply these principles to themselves, this is the time, this is the country, we my fellow-citizens are that nation. The war between the United States and France is not merely necessary and just and beneficial; a war not only for our property, our independence and sovereignty; but for our manners, our morality, our religion; for all we enjoy, for all we hope. Let the sons of Gaul beware.

Endnotes

1. http://www.pragmatism.org/american/witherspoon_grads.html.

2. http://books.google.com/books?id=kdDRJLxBhl4C&pg=PA103 &lpg=PA103&dq= John+Witherspoon,+1787&source=bl&ots=aTe8bB4tX- &sig=Qs7PUaI4nFa1JWNv-iFaMM10iQ0&hl=en&ei=aB7YSfjyLun plQeYm_ThDA&sa=X&oi=book_result&ct=result&resnum=7#PPA1 64,M1.

3. http://www.wholesomewords.org/missions/biobrainerd7.html.

4. Stile's biographer Edmund Morgan writes: "Since [Stiles's] congregation included several merchants and sea captains, he occasionally had the opportunity to invest a little extra cash in one of their voyages. . . . His most significant investment of this kind was in 1756, before he married. In that year he put a hogshead of rum (106 gallons) aboard a ship commanded by Captain William Pinnegar and bound for Guinea on the coast of Africa. Captain Pinnegar brought him back a ten-year-old Negro boy, to whom he gave the name 'Newport.'"

5. 13 F. Cas. 840 (C.C.E.D. Pa. 1833).

6. James King Morse, *Jedidiah Morse, A Champion of New England Orthodoxy* (New York: Columbia University Press, 1939), 95.

7. Wilfred H. Munro, *Picturesque Rhode Island*, 1881, 107–9.

8. Ibid, 107.

9. Henry L. Bowden, and Tristam Burges, *Memoir of Tristam Burges: With Selections from His Speeches and Occasional Writings* (Marshall, Brown, 1835), 14.

10. Bowden, 28.

11. Bowden, 36.

12. Edward Field, *State of Rhode Island and Providence Plantations at the End of the Century: A History* (Boston: Mason Publishing Co., 1902), vol 2, 424–30.

13. *Papers of the American Slave Trade, Series A: Selections from the Rhode Island Historical Society.*